Non-Violence in the World Religions

Non-Violence
in the World Religions

Vision and Reality

Hagen Berndt

scm press

Translated by John Bowden from the German *Gewaltfreiheit in den Weltreligionen, Vision und Wirklichkeit,* published 1998 by Gütersloher Verlag, Gütersloh.

0 334 02803 5

This edition first published 2000 by
SCM Press
9–17 St Albans Place London N1 0NX

SCM Press is a division of
SCM-Canterbury Press Ltd

Typeset by Regent Typesetting, London
Printed in Great Britain by
Biddles Ltd, Guildford and King's Lynn

'Each has a goal towards which he turns.
But emulate one another in good works.
Wherever you are,
God will bring you all together'

Qur'an, Surah 2, 148

CONTENTS

INTRODUCTION

In 1993 the peace researcher Johann Galtung gave a comprehensive description of violence as 'the avoidable infringement of basic human needs or, more generally, life, which puts the real degree of satisfying needs below what is potentially possible'. This pioneering statement on the theme of violence contains two words which can demand our whole attention, perhaps for life: 'possible' and 'avoidable'. The examples given in this book show us that far more is possible in this sphere than we dream of. They come from many lands and cultures with different situations of conflict. Many of the individuals from the world religions portrayed here had concrete utopias and dreams which by now have become reality.

The second word indicates that an infringement of basic needs is avoidable. So it is a matter of reflecting on a non-violent world just as much as on a better life – for all. This is a goal which challenges us to concentrate all our intelligence, our creativity, our bodily and physical strength on the possibility of peace. According to Galtung, peace in the sense of social justice and the implementation of human rights is far more than the absence of war. It is the absence of direct and structural violence. Galtung also adds 'cultural violence' which justifies direct or structural violence: scholarship, language, symbols or even religion can serve this end.

Therefore non-violence does not simply mean refraining from direct violence, nor does it mean inactivity. Non-violence means the effort to create justice and restore relationships without new violence. Here conflicts – interpersonal, social, international – can be understood as opportunities to work on injustice or an imbalance of power. Non-violent action arises out of taking responsibility for conflicts and gaining awareness that there is no ethically defensible and effective alternative. We will never be able to achieve absolute non-violence in our lifetimes – to claim the opposite would be naïve and possibly would disguise the actual situations of violence. Therefore non-violent action refers to the goal and means for achieving that goal which are in harmony with it.

Discussion of the sources and experiences of spiritual non-violence in the world religions of Judaism, Christianity, Islam, Hinduism and Buddhism can counter the misuse of religion to justify violence. However, no one can deny that all the religions mentioned have time and again become the instrument of violence and have had aspects which have prompted believers to acts of violence. They still do so today. A critical discussion with religious institutions, or institutions with a religious legitimation, which go along with violence is necessary. However, this should not be a 'clash of civilizations' from the outside; rather, it should be a discussion between members of each religion together with those who dialogue in solidarity with them.

This book presents contemporary witnesses and themes from the broad spectrum of non-violent action in the world religions. However, it is also part of a process of the appropriation of a world tradition, an ecumenical tradition in the original sense of the word, namely one which embraces the whole globe. Here ecumene is understood in the sense of the globe, the inhabited earth, and not just as contact between different Christian confessions.

The book is divided into two parts. Part One shows through short biographies what role non-violence has played and still plays in the thought and life of individuals. It is not a matter of making individuals heroes or heroines, for non-violent action aims to motivate and encourage people in different situations. The selection of these persons is subjective, but not fortuitous. As well as more well known figures, some others are introduced whose work has so far gone unnoticed by the media. Not all of them have used the term 'non-violence' in the sense in which I have explained it. Nevertheless, I have included them if their thought or action has made a substantial contribution to the development of non-violent visions or action. A brief glance at the table of contents will indicate that in this book women are in a minority; the reason for this is the incompleteness of the sources and the difficulty of gaining access to them. Christianity, the religion which has left the greatest mark on Western culture, is represented most strongly. This is not because it has the greatest tradition of non-violence. Such strong representation offers, rather, the opportunity to engage in a critical discussion of the Christian tradition of non-violence, which has often remained largely unknown to both Christians and non-Christians.

Part Two contains chapters on some central terms which have become important in non-violent movements. Religious thought reacts to the challenges of particular places and times. Therefore reflection on practice is the way in which new insights are opened up into the relationship between non-violent action and religion. In this sense the book is also meant to prompt other personal 'experiments with the truth'.

This book cannot be more than a beginning, nor is it meant to be. It is a stimulus towards more extended studies on the relationship between non-violent action and individual religions, interfaith dialogue, and its sources, which provide a basis for non-violent action. It also indicates the difficulties and limitations of non-violence.

I want to thank Gütersloher Verlagshaus most warmly for its readiness to publish this book. Without the collaboration, encouragement and patience of its editor, Christa Dommel, to whom I am deeply indebted, it would never have been written. I have also experienced quite exceptional patience from my wife Sepalika and our children Yunus, Arpana and Amrita, and from my colleagues in the Centre for Non-Violent Action.

I. Non-Violence in the Life of Individuals – Portraits

JUDAISM

Joseph Abileah

The army doesn't protect people

'All the people I've met in Israel know Joseph Abileah. They know that he is a conscientious objector and what he thinks about the Jewish-Arab Confederation.'

So remarked Jim Forrest, the former General Secretary of the International Fellowship of Reconciliation. Abileah, who was born in Austria in 1915, died in 1994 after more than fifty years of public pacifist action in Israel. The violinist Yehudi Menuhin, who was a friend of his, once described him as 'a fragile person, unarmed and vulnerable, but spiritually and intellectually strong, opposing tanks, poison gas and gas ovens, as a whole series of our fellow Jews have already done'.

Abileah came to Palestine in 1926. It was a time when the Palestinian Arabs were opposing not only British colonial rule but also the Jewish settlement of the land. One day Abileah met an Arab underground group which had instructions to kill Jews. Abileah calmly faced the group and said that the men should do what they had to do. He voluntarily went to the well into which they wanted to throw him. As no one was ready to do the deed, the Arabs defined him as a Muslim and so evaded their orders. Abileah, who had acted without much thought, later recognized that his only chance had lain in this gesture and not in the vain fight of an individual against superior forces.

Subsequently he also refused to join the Jewish brigade which the British Mandate authorities built up against a German attack on Palestine. This exposed him to criticism and pressure from those around him, so he moved from Haifa to Jerusalem. He did not believe that Fascism could effectively be opposed with armed force, but was convinced that viable changes come about through political and social measures. Therefore Abileah also did not join the Israeli army which was being recruited in preparation for the foundation of the State.

After the founding of Israel in 1948 his continued conscientious objection to serving in the army involved him in legal proceedings in which he had occasion to describe his attitude to the state and the army: 'These people are not defending me and my family. They cannot do that at all, because they are only defending an institution called a state. The state has been founded to give me security, and here it has failed. It is not only Israel which cannot do this. No state in the world can guarantee the life of its citizens.' Abileah pointed out that, in the wars of the twentieth century, to an increasing degree – in the 1980s up to ninety per cent – the victims have been civilians and that therefore it is impossible to say that soldiers protect the population. As the army had not wanted to have him after his appearances in public, Abileah was given permits which postponed his conscription for reasons of health. He gained legitimate exemption and was recognized as a conscientious objector. He refused alternative service in the army, but emphasized that he wanted to be active for the welfare of society. finally he was given a postponement of conscription which was extended annually.

Joseph Abileah also adopted positions critical of the system in the conflict with the Arabs. In 1946 he deleted the term 'Jew' from his passport and substituted 'Semitic'. He said of his religious allegiance that he was a 'monotheist', including in this term Christians and Muslims. Abileah learned much from Christian pacifists and orientated himself on the Sermon on the Mount in the New Testament. For him the ethical teaching of the Jew Jesus was not in contradiction with Jewish faith: 'It was merely a summary of ideas which were alive at that time. Therefore it is no problem for me to accept the Sermon on the Mount as a guideline for practising my Jewish faith. If I am asked about my religion I reply that I try to practise Jewish ethics as they were lived out by the first Christian communities.' He described this faith which he tried to live out as a complete Judaism, as a return to the roots of faith.

This man, who for many years played first violin in the Haifa Symphony Orchestra, was active on the executive committee of War Resisters International from 1957 to 1969. He kept arguing that nation states could give no lasting security and that a cultural survival of both Jews and Palestinians did not depend on whether there was an Israeli or a Palestinian state. On the contrary, religious ties which had held the Jews together in the Diaspora were becoming weaker in Israel because there was less need to stress one's own religious identity. Therefore Abileah argued for a confederation with Jordan, which he had got to know on his journeys in the colonial period.

In 1970 he reported to the UN Commission on Human Rights on the discrimination practised by the Israeli administration of the occupied West Bank. For this he was first attacked in the Israeli press and received threats. Then, however, the reporting shifted and he was praised for his objective arguments at a time when the Israeli government did not want to collaborate with the Human Rights Commission.

Joseph Abileah died in Haifa in 1994.

Literature

Anthony Bing, *Israeli Pacifist: The Life of Joseph Abileah*, Syracuse, NY: Syracuse University Press.

Halina Birenbaum

Contemporary witness of the Holocaust

'I was now closer to the mass extermination and could no longer deceive myself or stubbornly insist, "It's impossible." I began to lose my faith in life, in its constancy and its value, and even more in the possibility of ever leaving this hell again. For hundreds of thousands of people perished, although – as people were whispering in the camp – the Germans were staring final defeat in the face. I also lost my faith in people and the last remnant of respect. I was taciturn, silent and constantly irritable. I could no longer find any common language with anyone. I saw talk as meaningless in the face of the vileness of the world in which we live; in the face of the unatoned crime which we experienced daily as eyewitnesses; and in the face of the indifference of the imprisonment to all that did not concern us directly. Despite my spiritual collapse and my desperation, I never stopped smuggling things . . .'

Halina Birenbaum experienced this severe crisis as a fourteen-year-old girl during her imprisonment in the concentration camp of Auschwitz. She was born in 1929, the child of a lower-middle-class family in Warsaw. When she was ten years old the German army occupied Poland, and a year later the German occupying forces built the Warsaw ghetto, in which the Jewish population of the city and many deportees had to live in wretched conditions. At the latest in the spring of 1943 they were dragged off to other concentration camps, where most of them died in gas chambers or from hunger, forced labour, sickness or pseudo-scientific experiments. Halina Birenbaum was brought to Maidanek and until she was freed lived there, in Auschwitz, in Ravensbrück and in Neustadt-Glewe. Apart from her, only her oldest brother survived the Holocaust.

Halina Birenbaum was liberated in 1945. She returned to her birthplace, Warsaw, to go to school there, but only two years later emigrated to Israel and worked on a kibbutz. Questions of daily life in the new society of Israel came to the fore. It was the Eichmann trial that first brought her back into contact with her childhood. Suddenly she became aware that she had a past and a family. 'My loved ones, all their past, and my past with them, their life and their death were no longer shut away in me. It was as if they were living again in my presence.' Halina Birenbaum began to write her history. In an undogmatic, precise and sensitive way she describes her childhood in German concentration camps in her most important book, *Hope is Last to Die*. She describes the hopes which are shattered time and again, the battle for survival, the wish to maintain her dignity as a human being under humiliating circumstances. She also describes the complicity of prisoners with the murderers, the constant bafflement of threatening situations, the ceaseless confrontation with the suffering and death of relatives and friends. She attempts to prevent getting privileges to the detriment of others. Whenever she opposes the guards and the SS she experiences her power. She is also amazed at this in others, for example in the case of a Polish woman doctor who despite the threat of the death penalty tells a commission of the International Red Cross what the conditions in the concentration camp are really like.

Halina Birenbaum openly mentions the crime and the perpetrators, and at the same time continues to differentiate. After an operation on New Year's Day 1945 for a gunshot wound which was inflicted on her by a bored guardpost in Auschwitz-Birkenau, she comments on the visit of the doctor who examined her. 'Despite everything I was worried. A Nazi examines the sick in the name of order and discipline. But another, with the same principles in his head, condemns people to death. Both perform their tasks precisely and unerringly.'

The report which she keeps presenting to groups of young people and adults in Israel and Poland is particularly impressive in the way in which she describes her experience without any hatred. Halina Birenbaum gives her reports because in this way she is creating access to herself: 'Everything down to the smallest detail remains unquenched and fresh in my memory, as if it happened only yesterday. In the night I am visited by terrible dreams of persecution. In my sleep, together with my mother or a group of female prisoners I often seek hiding places and refuges, from Nazi bandits who are on our track.' But she also tells her story so that others may not forget, so that such crimes are not repeated. Here her testimony becomes an important contribution to reconciliation, which can take place only in this way, by disclosing and describing the burdensome events and crimes of the past. In deep faith in the positive possibilities of human beings, like other survivors she also talks about the Holocaust with young Germans.

Literature

Halina Birenbaum, *Hope is Last to Die: A Personal Documentation of Nazi Terror*, Oswiecim: Publishing House of the State Museum 1994.

Martin Buber

Proclaiming the perfect human being

'You must not hold back! You, who have entered the shells in which society, state, church, school, business, public opinion and your own arrogance have put you, not directly connected with anyone or anything else, break through your shell, become direct, and as a human being touch human beings!'

This call made by the Jewish writer and philosopher Martin Buber, which he published in 1919 at a time when his life was taking new directions, marks the end of a mystical phase of turning away from the world and a move towards reality. But until his death in Jerusalem in 1965, Buber's life continued to be governed by a mysticism of encounter and dialogue with other people. Still in 1916, a few years before the text quoted at the beginning, Buber's friend the anarchist Gustav Landauer had sharply criticized the philosopher for his support of German war policy: '. . . I say that you have no right – towards yourself – to talk publicly about the political events of the present which people call world war and classify these confusions in your beautiful and wise generalizations. What emerges is quite inadequate and infuriating.'

However, at that time Buber's 'conversion', as he later described the shift in his life, was already on the way. The decisive event was the visit of a young man who in 1914 'had come to me not by chance but by fate, not for applause, but for a decision. He had come especially to me, at this particular hour.' Buber describes how soon afterwards he learned that this man was no longer alive. At that point he first became aware that, despite his attentiveness in the conversation, he had not been fully devoted to someone in need. That day saw the beginning of his move to the religion of everyday life, responsibility and dialogue. Buber took the way to a deeper mysticism than that which is about ecstatic feelings of the individual.

Martin Buber was born in Vienna in 1878 but largely grew up in Lviv in present-day Ukraine and on his family's Polish estates. There in his youth he came into contact with Jewish Hassidism, that charismatic and worldly pietistic movement which had come into being in Eastern Europe in the eighteenth century and was characterized by a style of life which sought to reach God in love for fellow human beings. At the same time the way in which the educated Poles were rooted in German culture left its stamp on him: although in the last decades of his life he also wrote books in Hebrew, German was to be the language in which he developed and composed the most important thoughts of his long career. Buber studied in Vienna, Leipzig, Berlin and Zurich.

In his student days Martin Buber became a supporter of the Zionist movement, but clearly had different emphases from those of its founder Theodor Herzl. For Buber the idea of a 'Jewish state' was at first a distant utopia – he was concerned with the spiritual rebirth of Judaism, the development of a Jewish way of life and the formation of a strong community. At the latest a year before Herzl's death in 1904 he broke with the statesman; Herzl always had the real Palestine in view. Buber first moved there in 1938 when the pressure in Nazi Germany made any other decision inconceivable. He had apparently long been under the illusion that the obstacles to Jewish life were only transient and that a renewal of Jewish education and upbringing would contribute towards helping the Jewish community in Germany to survive. Right up to the destruction of his home he himself hoped to be able to work in two places, in Germany and in Palestine.

Buber's break with Herzl and partial retreat from Zionist politics coincided with the beginning of his interest in mystical traditions, especially his use of Hassidic spirituality, which to some degree he brought up to date. Through his publications the religious experiences of the Jews of Eastern Europe were preserved for posterity shortly before they were exterminated. Moreover his texts inspired the non-violent and pacifist Jewish movements in North America and in Israel.

However, in these first years of the twentieth century, in which other spiritual currents with a mystical stamp were widely accepted, Buber was initially concerned with the mediaeval German mystics, and then also with similar ideas from other cultures. It was only slowly, after years of fascination with mysticism, that Buber returned to that concern with everyday life which Hassidism thought so particularly important. From the end of the First World War he was occupied in adult education and devoted himself to a task which he set himself, namely, to make known the idea of the 'perfect human being' and to work towards this educational goal. The philosophical basis for his practice of educative dialogue, which in fact has a significance going far beyond education, is provided by the ideas which he presented in his book *I and Thou*, published in German in 1923. By means of the terms 'I-Thou' and 'I-It' Buber describes the need for true communication, engaging in dialogue with the other person in order to become authentically human, instead of just speaking and knowing about an object. 'The relationship to the Thou is immediate. All real life is encounter. The Thou encounters me by grace – it is not found by searching. Love is the responsibility of an I for a Thou. The creation reveals its form in encounter.'

From now on the realization of this I-Thou relationship is one of the determinative themes in Buber's life. It played a role in his divided relationship to Zionism – he opposed the violence used on the Arab population of Palestine – and also shaped his views on the difficult resumption of relations with post-war Germany. His commitment to human rights and a peaceful understanding with the Palestinians, his support of Arab women students, the conversations with Germans – all this made Buber a controversial person in Israel and for a long time caused him difficulties in accepting the state of Israel as his own.

Martin Buber's criticism of Zionist 'worshippers of violence' did not prevent him from contradicting Mahatma Gandhi's interpretation of non-violence in the face of the Holocaust. Prompted by an article of Gandhi's on the 'Situation of Jews in Germany and Palestine', Buber published his 'Letter to Gandhi': 'There is a situation in which no *satyagraha* of the power of truth can come into being from the *satyagraha* of the strength of the soul. The word *martyrium* means testimony; but what if there is no one there to receive the testimony? Such testimony is given; but who may require it?'

In his letter Buber makes it clear that the parallel which Gandhi draws between the situation of the Indian population of South Africa and the Jews in Germany is too simple; he emphasizes that the historical situations are fundamentally different. Certainly there are Jews who have shown strength of soul through their behaviour, But in this case Buber does not think that *satyagraha* is effective. However, this does not mean that the Jewish tradition approves of violence: '. . . from earliest times we have proclaimed the doctrine of justice and peace; we have taught and learned that peace is the goal of the world and that righteousness is the way to it. So we cannot want to use violence.' Therefore in Palestine Buber wants a balance between the equally justified Jewish and Arab claims to the land to be achieved through reconciliation: 'We should also be able to fight for justice, but fight in a loving way!'

Buber writes of himself: 'I am not a radical pacifist; I do not believe that one has to answer violence with non-violence everywhere. I know tragedy by sight.' Although Buber's attitude to the question of violence is ambivalent, his thought has made a direct contribution to the development of non-violent action in the modern Jewish world. Martin Buber encouraged models which call for relationship instead of domination, which expect from

Israel a different communal quality from that of a normal state, and which require a revival of old Jewish values.

Literature

Marc H.Ellis, *Toward a Jewish Theology of Liberation*, Maryknoll, NY: Orbis Books and London: SCM Press 1987.

Murray Polner and Naomi Goodman (eds), *The Challenge of Shalom. The Jewish Tradition of Peace and Justice*, Philadelphia: New Society Publications 1994.

Natan Hofshi

A political morality without violence

'The Jews as a whole had a special fate. Whatever evil people thought it appropriate to do to any people, even to a people which has never raised arms against them, they will certainly do to the Jews. The Jews seem to stand outside the law; they are not even regarded as human. This shocking phenomenon requires a thousand times more research than has been devoted to it so far. It is even more oppressive to think how this has led the Jews to the deceptive belief that they can solve their problem "like any other nation" by means of violence.'

Natan Hofshi, who formulated these ideas in 1942, explains them with examples from Jewish history in which positive decisions made from a belief in the liberating power of violence have led to even greater destruction. The renunciation of violence as a political means has at least had no worse consequences in the history of the Jews. With this attitude, particularly in the years of the extermination of the European Jews by the National Socialists, Hofshi belonged to a small minority which had often to suffer accusations of treachery.

The pacifist Natan Hofshi was born in Poland in 1889. There he had an Orthodox Jewish upbringing. The Zionism which was coming into being deeply impressed the young Hofshi, so that in 1909 he emigrated to Palestine. There he earned his living first as an itinerant agricultural worker. Through regular contact with Arabs he became aware of their problematical relationship to the immigrant Jews. When influential Jewish circles exerted pressure to dismiss Arab agricultural workers and from then on to give the land only to Jews to cultivate, in the 1930s growing Arab unrest led to a revolt. This was countered with the formation of militant Jewish groups. In this situation Hofshi called for more sensitivity to the interests of the Arab inhabitants of Palestine and rejected any course which made it necessary to arm the Jews. In the long term he saw greater chances of realizing Zionist goals through agreement and co-existence with the Arabs. But there were acts of violence on both sides.

Hofshi rejected this: 'Let us choose the right way before it is too late. Let us not soil our pure undertaking with fresh blood. We will carry on our just fight indefatigably, but wisely; without capitulating, but preserving our purity; resolutely, but not aggressively; with unyielding steadfastness, but not with abhorrent acts of murder or bloodshed.' In a situation in which the argument for a Jewish home state and thus for security for the Jews was also put forward with armed force and generally accepted, Hofshi found himself in a minority, which argued with great courage for another political morality.

Influenced by Tolstoy and Gandhi, he argued for a war of liberation with non-violent means. For him, as a fundamental notion of Jewish faith, respect for human life was the supreme goal. Natan Hofshi regarded power which springs from violence as incompatible with Jewish ideals. This attitude was reflected both in his personal life – he was a vegetarian – and also in his public demands during the various phases of the origin of Israel.

In addition, time and again he quotes images from the Hebrew Bible to describe how the Jews and Arabs are brothers and sisters. Jewish terrorism against the Arabs would brand all the Jews with the mark of Cain. Finally, violence against their Palestinian brothers would also affect relationships between Jews – Hofshi feared attacks on the small group of pacifists. 'The greatest danger comes from our own ranks,' he writes at the end of the 1930s, in the certainly that the war of liberation against British occupation would ultimately be successful. The 'weapons of Esau' (see Gen. 27.41ff.) would finally also be turned against Jews.

Natan Hofshi, who strongly influenced the Israeli pacifists active today, died in 1980.

Jeremy Milgrom

Rabbi for human rights

At a roadblock in the eastern part of Jerusalem soldiers were stopping the bus with Arab plates. They got in and asked for permits. Three or four young men, Palestinians, were taken out because they had none. Perhaps they had quickly hidden their permits because otherwise it would have become clear that they had come to Jerusalem from the West Bank or Gaza without military permission. Perhaps they had simply left their passes at home, as a protest against being treated as second-class citizens. They had to stand in front of a wall with hands raised high while they were being searched. Rifles were at the ready. In the bus the passengers, both Jews and Palestinians, were silent. While some were still wondering what would happen to these young men, an Israeli, dressed simply, got out and went slowly over to the soldiers. He talked to them, and managed to get the Palestinians on board the bus again to continue their journey. Israeli soldiers have respect for a rabbi. They trust him. It was Jeremy Milgrom. He supports human rights, regardless of what religion or nationality people belong to.

Jeremy Milgrom was born in the USA in 1953 and grew up in a family which had such great respect for the Jewish religion and Jewish education that only Hebrew was spoken at home. Israel was always being talked about in his family: when he was eight years old Milgrom's parents had a study year there. Some years later he won a Bible scholarship and was therefore able to finish his schooling in Jerusalem. As a fifteen-year-old, Milgrom felt very attracted to Orthodox Judaism. Therefore after his three years of military service he began to study Judaism and became a rabbi.

On his first appointment, to Galilee, Milgrom got an insight into Arab culture and began to become interested in interfaith encounter – there were many Palestinian villages around the place where he lived. But a deeper change in his thinking only came later, when his first daughter was born in 1982, a few years before the beginning of the war in Lebanon. He began to recognize the value of a human being in his child and refused to serve as a soldier in Lebanon. Only after eight years grappling with this conscientious decision was he allowed to cease to bear arms and was released from the reserve.

This also made it necessary for him to redefine his role as a rabbi. He recalls the Palestinian Anglican priest Shehadeh Shehaded, who when appointed had preached that he was the priest for everyone, not just for the Anglicans in the village. Shehadeh became his model. Jeremy Milgrom stopped being exclusively a rabbi for Israelis and became rabbi as a social resource for all. At this time he also met the peace activist Amos Gvirtz, who saw himself as a Jewish Israeli and at the same time as an atheist. On the basis of this encounter Milgrom began to see his

protest against discriminatory policies and military violence from
the aspect of non-violence: previously it had been political. Like
many non-violent activists of his generation he found support
here in the writings of Thomas Merton. Jeremy Milgrom says that
Christian sources of non-violence influence him more strongly
than purely Jewish ones.

Nevertheless, Milgrom believes that non-violence accords with
Jewish thought and faith: 'A basis for religious humanism is
the idea that there is a divine spark in every human being. This
doctrine is based on Gen.5.1, where it is said that in principle
human beings are created in the image of God. Therefore the
subsequent focus in the Bible on the Israelites and the Jewish
emphasis on a unique agreement between God and the Jews
cannot diminish our obligation to create a comprehensive human
community. No theology which did this could claim authenticity
for itself.'

Jeremy Milgrom rejects as ethnocentricity the special status
which some Jewish circles claim for themselves today and in individual instances even uses the term racism. Certainly he understands the reasons which have led to the formation of these
attitudes: in antiquity the outsider status in the 'pagan' environment of a community with a monotheistic stamp, the segregation
and persecutions in a later time, the experience of the Holocaust in
the twentieth century and the formation of a political elite in Israel
and in the USA. However, he points out that present-day life in an
open, pluralistic society does not justify polemic which rejects
others: 'Jews are fully justified in reclaiming for themselves
humanistic sensibilities which have been preserved in Christian or
Muslim texts and are less burdened by the experiences of persecution and exile.'

Milgrom does not understand why today more Jews who have
been brought up in a humanistic tradition with a sense of justice
do not feel drawn to non-violence. For even in the everyday life of
a Jew, respect for the value of every life plays a role; it is expressed

and communicated, for example, by the food laws. In Milgrom's family, above all among the children, this has developed into a vegetarian lifestyle. Jeremy Milgrom has a lot of time for Maimonides' description of Jewish justice: 'Do not inflict suffering on anyone, be persecuted rather than persecute, insulted rather than insult; of a man who lives in this way scripture says, "Israel, my servant, I have chosen you" (Isaiah).'

In this sense Milgrom's organization Rabbis for Human Rights attempts to return to the original task and vision of serving human beings in their diversity out of religious conviction, instead of helping just a small group to establish itself. Since the middle of the 1990s Jeremy Milgrom has been involved in securing the rights of the Jahalin, a small Arab nomadic tribe which was to give way to a new Jewish settlement east of Jerusalem. His encounter with these Arabs, from whom he learned to value the real shepherd's life, also raised theological questions for Milgrom about his understanding of himself as a Jew.

If the Jahalin were Jews, then they would have regarded Israeli society as pioneers in implementing a divine plan for the settlement of the Holy Land. Therefore the political controversy with the Jahalin also reflects a theological conflict, the outcome of which will determine whether Israel will develop into a secure and stable society by respecting human rights. Milgrom defines his task as follows: 'As rabbis we are called on to bring both daily life and the visions of a future into accord with Jewish ideals and values. We understand the thorough process through which our society assigns the land and its blessings exclusively to the Jews; we have read and taught the same texts, which describe the importance of the land as a sign of the treaty between God and the people. But we cannot let the manifest meaning of these texts become the basis for discrimination.' He sets the ideology of segregation as the most appropriate Jewish form of life over against Jewish experiences of harmonious co-existence with others. According to Milgrom, the insight that Jews were not the only victims of the Holocaust requires and makes possible the building up of trust and partnership with people of other traditions and religions who feel obligated to the same values of justice.

CHRISTIANITY

Carlos Filipe Ximenez Belo

Shepherd and advocate of his community

'At the risk of his life he sought to save his people from the onslaughts of those in power. With his efforts to bring a just solution to self-determination on the basis of the law of the people he has constantly supported non-violence and dialogue with the Indonesian authorities.'

Those were the reasons given by the Nobel Prize Committee on 11 October 1996 for awarding the Nobel Peace Prize to Bishop Carlos Filipe Ximenez Belo, a prize which he shared with Jose Ramos-Horta, the representative of the Timorese exiles. Carlos Belo spoke out clearly on the observance of human rights in East Timor, which has been occupied by Indonesia since December 1975 and was annexed in 1976. However, primarily he sees himself as pastor of his community in Dili, which since 1983 he has led as apostolic administrator.

The eastern part of Timor, a small island in South-East Asia not far from the north coast of Australia, had been a Portuguese colony for about 400 years when after the democratization of Portugal at the beginning of 1975 the independence movement developed there. The different parties were still fighting over the future of their land when in June 1975 the Communist Fretilin (Frente Revolucionaria de Timor Leste Independente) won the elections and soon afterwards declared independence.

Even though some East Timorese groups argued for a link with Indonesia, a large and neighbouring country – especially with a view to the economic development of the country, which had been much neglected by Portugal – there was a strong movement for autonomy: in contrast to Indonesia, which is predominantly Muslim, the majority of the inhabitants of East Timor are Catholic. The Pacific-Melanesian population of the island does not feel that it is represented by the Malay tradition of the ruling population in Indonesia. Therefore the annexation by Indonesia led to a war of liberation. The violent occupation of the country cost about a third of the population their lives and could be maintained only at great military cost and with constant violation of human rights. In this situation Bishop Belo, as the administrator of the diocese of Dili, was put directly under the Vatican and thus from then on was no longer attached to the Indonesian conference of bishops. In this situation he was constantly forced to tread a knife edge. After being abducted by young rebels who had been living in his residence shortly beforehand, he said: 'I must now face two sides: the soldiers who accuse me of supporting demonstrations, and the young people who accuse me of having sold them out to Indonesia, because I do not allow them to demonstrate in my residence.'

Carlos Belo was born in 1948, the child of a peasant family, near Baucau, the second largest city of East Timor. As his father had died early, his mother, who was regarded as being very pious, took over his education. At a very early stage he was interested in the life of the Italian priest Don Bosco and the Salesian Order which he founded. At the age of twenty Belo went to Portugal, there to study classical languages and later philosophy and theology. In 1974 he entered the Salesian Order, which enabled him to complete his studies in Rome in 1981. He was ordained priest in 1980. Belo returned to Baucau as assistant priest, and there became head of a priests' seminary.

However, very soon his situation was to change dramatically. In 1983 Bishop Martinho da Costa Lopez, the apostolic administrator of the diocese of Dili in East Timor, left the country and went into exile in Portugal. Previously on many occasions he had sharply criticized the violation of human rights by the Indonesian occupying forces and for that had been put under considerable pressure. He had also expressed his disappointment at the Catholic Church, since the Vatican had not taken a public stand on the persecution of the East Timorese.

It was generally assumed that under pressure from the Indonesian government the Vatican would want to hand over the leadership of the diocese to a less experienced and weaker person and that that was why the choice had fallen on Belo. He himself had not experienced the years of the Indonesian genocide on East Timor and seemed to be well disposed to Indonesia, since on taking office he had also had to assume Indonesian citizenship. For this reason most priests of East Timor boycotted his institution. In April 1988 Belo was consecrated bishop of the 'titular diocese' of Lorium in Italy. That gave him the rank of bishop, which was his due, without the Vatican having to make a statement about the state allegiance of East Timor. For in this way the Catholics of the island remained directly attached to Rome and not to the church in Indonesia.

But Belo soon came into contact with the Indonesian conference of bishops and was able to assure himself of their solidarity and their understanding of the suffering of people in East Timor. Nevertheless Carlos Belo does not understand himself as a liberation theologian, but more as a priest who is compelled to take a stand: 'I speak as someone who has the responsibility to bear witness to what he has seen and heard, to react to what I know to be true, to keep the flame of hope alive, to do what is possible to warm the earth for another day. I speak as a spiritual leader, not as a politician, which in fact I am not.' Here it becomes clear how strongly rooted he is in the Christian model of prophetic witness – quite the opposite to a series of Asian non-violent figures, for whom striving for harmony comes first.

Belo's best-known statement is his letter to the UN Secretary-General Perez de Cuellar of 6 February 1989, a letter which was published only five years later by de Cuellar's successor. In this letter he writes the often-quoted sentence 'We are dying as a people' and therefore asks the Secretary-General to carry through the process of decolonization on Timor, i.e. to hold a referendum. Probably with this statement on the political status of the island Belo ventured too far, certainly too far for the Vatican. Today he speaks only of the right to self-determination, but largely leaves open how this is to be achieved politically. In his speech on being awarded the Nobel Peace Prize he explains the tasks of a bishop: 'His special mission is a spiritual one. He has a duty to engage in this mission as the giver of the spiritual sources for the salvation of men and women and to strengthen them in faith in Jesus Christ. But humankind is not limited to a spiritual dimension; one should be redeemed as a whole, as a human being and spiritually. In this respect a Catholic bishop can never remain indifferent if the possibilities of the people for realizing their humanity – in all its dimensions – are to be realized.'

This basic attitude of Belo's sometimes issues in very clear and harsh criticism of the Indonesian military, or also of foreign politicians for their trivialization of the situation of East Timor. For example, he spoke out after the massacre at the cemetery of Santa Cruz in November 1991, in which more than 200 people not only died from the bullets of the soldiers but were also murdered the following night in hospitals, prisons or hiding-places.

Belo, who is under close guard, conjectures that three times there have been attempts to murder him: in 1989, after the letter to the UN Secretary-General which has already been quoted; in 1991, when he visited the site of one of the great massacres of the civil population in 1983; and in 1996, after he had been awarded the Nobel Peace Prize. Nevertheless Belo is relaxed and cheerful. Time and again he seeks dialogue with the authorities and with the young people, to whom he has a good approach. He invites them to act thoughtfully and with an eye to the future. Bishop Kamphaus of Limburg writes of him: 'His door is open and so is his heart. His appearance is unpretentious, and precisely for that reason it is convincing. He can give people confidence.'

Literature

Paul Raffaele, 'Hero for a Forgotten People', *Readers Digest* (Australian and South-East Asian edition), March 1996.

'A Shepherd in the Midst of Suffering in East Timor', *The Nation*, Bangkok, 12 December 1996 (Belo's speech on being awarded the Nobel Peace Prize).

'Nobel Peace Prize a Victory for East Timor', *Tapol: The Indonesia Human Rights Campaign*, Bulletin 138, Surrey, December 1996 (further articles in this journal).

Dorothy Day

Identification with the poor

'I can say with all my heart that I loved the Communists with whom I worked and learned a lot from them. They helped me to find God in his poor people, in his forsaken ones, and I had not succeeded in doing this in the Christian church.' The spiritual life of the American Dorothy Day is shaped by her socialist view of the world and her Catholicism. The journalist and peace activist was born on 8 November 1897, the third of five children.

Initially religion played a part in her adolescent upbringing only through contact with pious neighbours: first Methodists, and then, after various moves by the family, also Catholics. Stimulated by these contexts, she experimented with an ascetic lifestyle and with piety. When she went as a young girl to Chicago, Dorothy Day soon came into contact with socialist thinking through her brother, who wrote about the situation of the workers, through her own reading, and on long walks through the social hot-spots of the city. These impressions, and her desire for economic independence from her parents, led her in 1916 to take a job as journalist with the socialist paper *The Call*. However, involvement in journalism was not enough for her; in 1918, also influenced by the World War in Europe, she began to train as a nurse. She wanted to work directly for the needy. Journalism and active love of neighbour – these are the two elements in the practical life of Dorothy Day.

With this motivation, in 1933, together with Peter Maurin, a French social critic whom she had got to know a few months earlier, she founded the first 'houses of hospitality'. For some time her home and at the same time the editorial rooms of the journal *The Catholic Worker*, which she had edited since 1 May 1933, had been staging-posts for many people in difficult situations. Therefore the houses of the non-violent Catholic left, above all in the USA but also in England, the Netherlands and in Germany, are known by the name of 'Catholic Workers House'.

The world economic crisis resulted in great impoverishment even in North America. In the houses of hospitality, of which thirty-three were opened in the first three years, the homeless could find somewhere to stay and the poor were given food. As early as 1937, the New York Catholic Workers House was feeding 400 people a day, and a year later twice as many. In this way Maurin and Day took seriously Jesus' command to serve one's neighbour, the stranger and the poor, and attempted to revive the mediaeval tradition of the hospice. In the fifth century bishops had established community centres which devoted themselves to social tasks, something which in modern times was still practised only by a few monasteries. Here Maurin, who had studied church

history, saw an opportunity for the churches and also for individual Christians.

Dorothy Day's own conversion to Catholicism took place by way
of many detours. The final impetus came from the birth of her
daughter in March 1926, which she experienced almost as a miracle.
Six years previously she had terminated an unwanted pregnancy
and for a long time had assumed that she would remain childless.
Her second pregnancy led her to occupy herself more intensively
with religion, so at the beginning of 1927 first the young child and a
few months later the thirty-year-old mother were baptized.

The judicial murder of the two anarchists Sacco and Vanzetti
fell in this period; it moved her deeply and she attempted to
explain it to herself in religious categories. 'The whole people was
mourning. By the whole people I mean the poor, the workers, the
trade unionists – those who had most intensively developed a
sense of solidarity. This is the same sense of solidarity which has
slowly helped me to understand the doctrine of the mystical body
of Christ, by which we become parts of one another.' This phase of
her life shaped the combination of Dorothy Day's social commitment with spiritual thinking.

Here her relationship with the church remained quite ambivalent. Certainly the Catholic Church was the only true church
for her, because of its universal claim and its particular power to
communicate to the masses. Nevertheless, even during the days
immediately after her baptism she came to wonder whether she
had betrayed the oppressed and the radical movement in favour of
a church which made a pact with the rich and with capitalism.
'How I longed for a synthesis which reconciled body and soul, this
world and the world to come.'

Dorothy Day first experienced this reconciliation by editing
The Catholic Worker and then much later, when between 1963
and 1965 she travelled to Rome for the Second Vatican Council
and saw from a distance Pope John XXIII, who embodied many
of her efforts for the renewal of the church. Like Hildegard

Goss-Mayr (see below, 33–7), with whom she worked in Rome, she was a member of the Fellowship of Reconciliation, in whose US branch she had been working since 1929, the only Catholic woman among Protestants. Pacifism was also a dominant theme in the first decade of *The Catholic Worker*. In her journal Dorothy Day opposed preparations for war, Fascism and antisemitism, even in the Catholic Church. Demonstrations in front of the German Embassy, campaigns for the unrestricted immigration of Jews and against the political relations of the USA with the Franco regime in Spain, which was legitimating itself with the help of the church, cost the journal as many subscribers as its explicitly pacifist stance after the United States' entry into the war. Many sympathizers thought that now it was necessary to fight. The number of the unemployed declined with the development of the war industry, so that Catholic Workers Houses lost support and many of them had to be closed. But Dorothy Day stuck to Jesus' love of enemy and the principle of 'peace without victory' which she had learned from Francis of Assisi.

Dorothy Day orientated herself not only on the Bible, especially the Sermon on the Mount, but also on the mediaeval mystics. Teresa of Avila was her great model and she identified with her: Teresa was regarded as a reformer in sixteenth-century Spain and as the founder of religious communities. There were also many parallels in the personal life of the two women: the frequent journeys, the poverty, the profession of inconvenient truths. Dorothy Day spent part of her time in prayer and adopted poverty as a presupposition for her own freedom.

In later years she was impressed by the fight of the agricultural workers for better working conditions. With their leader Cesar Chavez, whose attempts to organize the workers from 1965 on she actively supported, she shared a radical commitment which had a Christian motivation. She felt at home in the circles of the workers, who predominantly came from the Catholic societies of Mexico or the Philippines.

As a result of her involvement in a strike of farm workers, in summer 1973, for the last time in her life, she went to prison; she died on 29 November 1980. Spells in prison had been an important experience for her. She had suffered her first imprisonment as a twenty-year-old activist campaigning for votes for women. After only a few days she doubted whether being in prison made sense; it had been meant to make the public aware of the issue of the vote, but in principle its theme was not violence and injustice. However, here she met prisoners who were serving time for crimes for which they saw the whole of society and themselves responsible. This experience of deep identification never left her: 'I was the mother whose child had been raped and murdered. I was the mother who had given birth to the monster who had done this. I myself was the monster, feeling all the abhorrence in my breast.'

Literature

Jim Forrest, *Love Is the Measure. A Biography of Dorothy Day*, Maryknoll, NY: Orbis Books 1954.
Dorothy Day, *The Long Loneliness*, New York: Harper and Row 1972.

Adolfo Pérez Esquivel

Co-ordinator of solidarity

'Contrary to his own intentions, at a time when our land was occupied in the most intense armed battle against the terrorists, the activities of the architect Pérez Esquivel were exploited by others to safeguard the impunity of members of various terrorist groups. Therefore he had to be arrested and handed over to the national executive, in accord with the norms which apply in a state of emergency. As soon as the fighting stopped, the national executive decided to release him.' This was the comment by the Argentinian government on the decision of the Nobel Prize committee to award Adolfo Pérez Esquivel the Nobel Peace Prize in 1980. This was also the first official statement on the reasons for the imprisonment of the co-ordinator of the Latin American non-violent movement Servicio Paz y Justicia (SERPAJ, Service for Peace and Justice), which has a Christian background.

Adolfo Pérez Esquivel was born in Buenos Aires in 1931, the son of a Spanish immigrant. He went to predominantly Catholic schools, where he had a religious education which he later described as 'formal'. Already in his youth he came into contact with the writings of Mahatma Gandhi, Thomas Merton and the Order of the Little Brothers of Jesus founded by Charles de Foucauld. He was particularly impressed by Gandhi's interpretation of the Sermon on the Mount and Gandhi's remark that he would long since have become a Christian had the behaviour of Christians matched their own claims.

Already as a student at art college, Esquivel was involved in social neighbourhood projects in the suburbs of Buenos Aires with a group which had spiritual roots. This involvement deepened into more specific commitment to non-violence through contact with Lanza del Vasto, the founder of the L'Arche communities, who was visiting Argentina, and with Jean Goss and Hildegard Goss-Mayr.

Only at the end of the 1960s did Adolfo Pérez Esquivel's life change dramatically. The failed development policy of the Argentinian military regime led to an increase in politically moti-vated violence and, after the bloody suppression of unrest in 1969, to a guerrilla war. Pérez Esquivel rejected the violence on both sides. A year before this, the Second General Assembly of the Latin American episcopate had discussed in Medellín, Colombia, the pastoral reorientation of work in the Catholic communities of the individual countries against the background of the decrees of the Second Vatican Council. Individual bishops and parts of the lay movement in the churches of Latin America had long awaited this critical discussion of the historical position of the church, its responsibility for justice and social development, and its attitude to violence. Pérez Esquivel was also gripped by this sense of a new departure.

Whereas little note had been taken of a first consultation by the Christians interested in non-violence as a liberating force which was held in Montevideo, Uruguay, in 1966, in 1971 at a continental meeting in Costa Rica there were already reports on experiences of revolutionary non-violence from fifteen Latin American countries. A cautious beginning was made of co-ordinating these efforts, which in 1974 led to the appointment of Adolfo Pérez Esquivel to the SERPAJ office in Buenos Aires. For years Pérez Esquivel had recognized that the movement, which was still weak, needed mutual solidarity and exchanges in order to be able to act effectively. Now, after the International Fellowship of Reconcili-ation had been providing help for twelve years in bringing SERPAJ to birth through the work of Jean Goss and Hildegard Goss-Mayr, the Latin Americans took the issue of non-violence into their own hands.

Adolfo Pérez Esquivel again travelled a great deal through Latin

America; he spoke with church governments and lay movements, and supported movements among the poor. He knew that gentle social work had to be replaced with commitment at the grass roots for real justice. Often he suffered brief periods of imprisonment on his travels. But he had his most marked experience of state violence in 1977. The growing uncertainty over his work had already become evident soon after the further coup by the Argentinian generals: his office was ransacked. In April 1977 he was imprisoned for fourteen months and was then put under house arrest for a further fourteen months. His support for human rights and his work of organizing the poor were a thorn in the flesh of the military, who were dealing brutally with any opposition in their so-called 'dirty war' against the guerrillas. Pérez Esquivel probably avoided the fate of the many 'disappeared' of Argentina only because of the resolute activity of his wife Amanda. He found imprisonment and torture an important experience which strengthened his Christian attitude and motivation.

In prison Pérez Esquivel learned to resist and to maintain a fighting spirit despite difficult circumstances. He experienced that the spirit of freedom cannot be suppressed by state pressure and that self-control through prayer and meditation are important sources of strength. In solitary confinement and without any intellectual stimulation he had the possibility 'of hearing God's silence'. On the cell walls he discovered graffiti; of these the statement 'God does not kill' impressed him most deeply. In letters smuggled out of prison he grappled with Jesus' prayer 'Father, forgive them for they know not what they do.' At first it seemed to him that the doctors, officials and police involved in administering torture were very well aware of what they were doing. What they knew nothing of, however, Pérez Esquivel writes, was their own humanity, which they destroyed through the torture.

After his release Pérez Esquivel painted his well-known picture 'Christ in a Poncho', based on a vision which he had had on a journey to Ecuador. For him, Christ embodies a Christ of the poor

who promises them liberation. His declared aim was the procla-
mation of a word of God which brings about the liberation of men
and women as persons. Here he criticized the liberation theology
predominant in Latin America: in his estimation it had not yet
reflected sufficiently on non-violence. Non-violence has to replace
violence as an effective means with which the fight for justice is
carried on, and should also change everyday life.

The non-violence called for in Latin America is, however, in his
view different from that practised in Europe, which is concerned
only with individual conflicts and does not put the whole social
structure in question: 'Non-violence is not passivity or con-
formism. It is spirit and method. It is prophetic spirit, because it
condemns any split in the fellowship of brothers and sisters and
declares that this fellowship can be restored only through love.
And it is a method – an organized series of breaches in the civil
order, aimed at disrupting the system which is responsible for the
injustice all around us.'

Literature

Charles Antoine (ed.), *Adolfo Pérez Esquivel. Christ in a Poncho: Testimonials of the Nonviolent Struggles in Latin America*, Maryknoll, NY: Orbis Books 1983.
Philip McManus and Gerald Schlabach (eds), *Relentless Persistence: Nonviolent Action in Latin America*, Philadelphia: New Society Publishers 1991.

Hildegard Goss-Mayr

Powerful through the power of her soul

A twelve-year old girl is standing in the crowd of people along the street which has been marshalled for Hitler's visit to Vienna in 1942. Hitler arrives, the crowd is jubilant and all raise their hands in the Hitler greeting. Not the girl. All her life she will remember this event, her 'first conscious encounter with the demonic power of evil', as she writes in her autobiography. It will motivate her to engage in peace work and to seek the power of God in people and in history.

At that time Hildegard Goss-Mayr felt alone. Even today she still works alone, but radiates a strength which wins people over to her mission. Like her model Hildegard of Bingen, the mediaeval mystic, she bases her work for justice and liberation with the methods of active non-violence on a living Christian spirituality. At the latest from 1953, when at the age of twenty-three she completed her studies in philosophy, philology and history, Hildegard Goss-Mayr made the combination of mysticism with political and social commitment her task.

She was well prepared for it: her father, the Catholic pacifist Kaspar Mayr, was already working in the 1920s in the leadership team of the International Fellowship of Reconciliation, founded shortly before the First World War. The admonition not to counter hatred with hatred, but through love to lead people away from criminal thought and action, was one of the most important legacies of the father to his daughter Hildegard, who was born in Vienna.

After her marriage to the French opponent of war Jean Goss in 1958, Hildegard and Jean first visited Eastern Europe on behalf of the International Fellowship of Reconciliation, to work for reconciliation after the events of the Nazi period and the Second World War. Later Latin America, Asia and finally in the 1990s Francophone Africa were the goals of her commitment to a non-violent liberation from oppression and dictatorship. In 1991 Jean Goss died on the day of their departure for a seminar in Madagascar. Hildegard is continuing their joint work in Africa alone.

The powers of death and violence – a motif which keeps repeating itself with Hildegard Goss-Mayr – threatened to catch up with the young woman after the end of the Second World War. She fell into a deep crisis of existence and meaning which she only gradually overcame. How could she live on in a world in which all humanity had been betrayed, as it had been by Fascism and war? The power which became the basis of her life arose out of dedication with all her being to 'the service of liberating love' in order in this way to work in the power of the living Christian God for justice and human dignity, to oppose violence and destruction. The crucified Jesus, who overcame destruction and betrayal of human beings with the love of God, became Hildegard Goss-Mayr's most important model; it answered her question about the meaning of life and still supports her today.

Hildegard Goss-Mayr understands the task of human beings to take part in God's work of creation as a universal and radical challenge. For her, history is directed through the discovery and development of the power of the love of God present in men and women. Historical progress in the development towards a completely reconciled fellowship of men and women comes about when people devote themselves to overcoming oppression, discrimination and a lust for power and other demeaning limits, even in the face of resistance.

Hildegard Goss-Mayr and her husband Jean Goss were faced with this challenge from 1962 on, when they travelled to Latin America. For a good ten years that was to become the focal point of their work. Together they experienced the non-violent fight for liberation by a growing minority in the churches and around them, and helped in the foundation of the organization Servicio Paz y Justicia en America Latina (see p.29). They later described the experiences of the fight for liberation as a 'gift of the poor to the rich'. The poor called on the inhabitants of the rich countries to accept this gift, for they had lost patience in going along with the process of liberation slowly, They were convinced that fundamental changes were necessary both in the individual and in society. In particular Hildegard Goss-Mayr held a system based on economic growth and increased prosperity for a minority in the world responsible for the domination of dictatorships, oppression and terrorism in dependent regions. She claimed that in the industrial nations this led to feelings of meaninglessness and impotence, resignation and alienation from an authentic human self-determination.

In the course of their travels in almost all the countries of Latin America, she and Jean Goss took part in conferences, arranged seminars, and met representatives of the churches and revolutionary movements. They exposed themselves to the attacks of dictatorial regimes, as in 1975 on a visit to Brazil. When they returned there at the beginning of March 1975 from a seminary in Argentina they were arrested on arrival at the airport. Taken to a torture centre with black hoods over their heads, they were subjected to psychological torture and interrogated. After some days in prison, which they spent in prayer and fasting, they were released on the intervention of the Cardinal of São Paulo.

Hildegard Goss-Mayr addresses her demands for inner renewal quite specifically to the European churches. She expects the churches to take responsibility and show a readiness to become poor and free. For Hildegard Goss-Mayr, the basis for commitment to the 'mode of being of poverty' is the beatitude 'Blessed are you poor before God – yours is the kingdom of God' (Matthew 5.3). For her, radical repentance means freeing oneself from privilege and a desire to dominate in order to gain inner freedom in the face of unjust claims to power; to testify to the truth about injustice and dependence; to limit consumption; to choose an alternative lifestyle and to contribute in a non-violent way to establishing justice.

Since 1984 she has been communicating all this in training sessions and seminars – she speaks of 'schooling for the fight for liberation' – in the Philippines. These courses with members of religious orders, bishops and intellectuals of the opposition created an organized non-violent movement and the basis for the successful and non-violent rebellion against the dictatorial Marcos regime in Manila in February 1986. For Hildegard Goss-Mayr, the revolution provoked by the rigged elections at the beginning of February 1986 came too early. Many people, especially members of the rich middle class, were not prepared to follow up the political change with a social revolution. From this experience Hildegard Goss-Mayr derived the insight that the construction of a new society must be shaped programmatically in the early preparation phase of a political movement.

Looking back on her experiences with Jean Goss at the Second Vatican Council between 1961 and 1965, she feels ambivalent. Although her hopes of persuading the Catholic Church to make a clear statement against war and for a just peace were ultimately disappointed, at that time she succeeded, despite great opposition, in making war and peace the theme. However, Hildegard Goss-Mayr is recognizing late fruits of these efforts only today, for example in the rise of peace and shalom ministries at a time when she sees the achievements of the Council being suppressed by conservative forces in the church.

Literature

Hildegard Goss-Mayr, *Der Mensch vor dem Unrecht, Spiritualität und Praxis gewaltloser Befreiung,* Vienna: Europa Verlag 1976.

Hildegard Goss-Mayr, *Wie Feinde Freunde werden*, Freiburg: Herder Verlag 1996.

Martin Luther King

A modern disciple of Jesus Christ

'Peace is not when there are no obvious tensions but when justice rules. Today, when in Montgomery the oppressed are rising and beginning to concern themselves with a lasting positive peace, this tension is necessary. That is also what Jesus meant with his saying, "I have not come to bring peace, but a sword." By that Jesus definitely did not mean that he had come to bring a real sword but something like this. "I have come not to bring this old negative peace with its fatal passivity. I have come to crack the whip against such peace. When I come, there is fighting and conflict between the old and the new. When I come, justice and injustice part company. I have come to bring a positive peace in which justice and love dwell – indeed I have come to establish the kingdom of God.'"

For Martin Luther King Jr, Jesus Christ was the model in the battle for justice, a model which he continually cited, from which he regained his courage in difficult times and which he followed in his own life and death. Often he doubted whether his strength was sufficient, in the face of the threats to which he was exposed, to go on fighting for a peace with justice. Then he turned to his God and went the way that finally led to his murder. King's non-violence was neither harmless nor naïve, aimed only at giving the black middle class in the USA a share of power. From the middle of the 1960s King also opposed the Vietnam war, and towards the end of his life he supported the rights of exploited workers of whatever origin.

Martin Luther King was born in 1929 in Atlanta, Georgia. His father and other members of the family had already made a name for themselves in the struggle for equal rights for the coloured population of the southern US states. So as a child he not only experienced the effects of racial segregation but was also brought up with the awareness that it is necessary and possible to take active steps against it. However, initially, from 1944, he studied theology in order to become a preacher in a Baptist congregation, like his father and grandfather.

At the age of eighteen he once said to his father, who was worried about the political involvement of his son in a mixed student organization: 'I know that I could hate every single white and that would be easy. But that is precisely the point: it would be too easy, and I know that the answers to most of these questions are far more difficult.' Martin Luther King recognized that he had to act morally. But his conviction about non-violent action developed slowly, and became decisive only with his work in the Civil Rights Movement after 1955.

He laid the foundations for that during his study, when he read Thoreau on civil disobedience, grappled critically with Marx and other Communist classics, and listened to the pacifist A.J. Muste. Muste's ideas fascinated King, but he doubted the possibility of being able to establish non-violence in the face of repressive regimes. After a report by Mordecai Johnson on his visit to India, King was very influenced by Mahatma Gandhi. Even if this did not yet mark a breakthrough to a conviction about non-violence, he later wrote: 'At an early stage I had already recognized that Christ's teaching about love together with Gandhi's method of non-violence was one of the most powerful weapons in Gandhi's fight for freedom.' Only when King became exposed to acute threat during the bus boycott in Montgomery did he dispense with armed protection and put into practice the ideas about which he had read.

In 1954 Martin Luther King became pastor at Dexter Avenue

Baptist Church in Montgomery, Alabama, thus initially giving up plans to embark on an academic career. Already in the first months of his work as a preacher in Montgomery there were demonstrations and actions against racial segregation – with disappointing results: the city administration did not see itself compelled to change its politics, and the majority of the coloured population were resigned to their situation. This dynamic changed only when on 1 December 1955 the seamstress Rosa Parks refused to give up her seat in the bus to a white and was arrested. This was the beginning of the Montgomery bus boycott, which dragged on until 21 December 1956. For a year, the Afro-Americans in Montgomery refused to use public buses, went on foot, and organized private lifts. Then the US Supreme Court of Justice resolved to abolish racial segregation on public transport.

In the boycott, which was organized by activists of the NAACP (National Association for the Advancement of Colored People) and essentially by clergy of the black Protestant churches, King quickly rose to the head of the Montgomery Improvement Association (MIA), specially founded for the purpose. In this position King, who was a compelling speaker, showed skill in negotiation and organization. When the bus company and city administration saw their initial hope that the action would quickly die down disappointed, there were negotiations and attempts to split the car pool, and then legal proceedings were taken against it; there was also intimidation, and open threats were made against those involved in the boycott. King, who was exposed to threats particularly from the beginning of 1956, escaped a bomb attack at the end of January. The atmosphere in this early period prepared him inwardly for the threat to which he was continually exposed until his violent death on 4 April 1968 in Memphis, Tennessee.

Martin Luther King knew that an effective organization of the movement, confidence in its own structures, a policy of timely and good information, and the involvement of as many people as possible in decisions and discussions contributed to the success of a campaign which had been begun and supported by only a few activists. King once said that Gandhi, too, who moved all India, had only about 100 companions around him. This is also the context of the development of training methods for the non-violent resolution of conflicts – there is a need to practise new behaviour.

After the success of the Montgomery bus boycott, in 1957 King and others founded the Southern Christian Leadership Conference (SCLC), which had the initial aim of persuading the coloured population which hitherto had been excluded from elections to have themselves entered on the voting lists despite the public obstacles. The SCLC was to remain Martin Luther King's basic organization. However, from the beginning of the 1960s there were increasingly conflicts with the militant, partly nationalistic wings of the black movements. These groups organized themselves into the Black Power Movement, which wanted to end the domination of the whites with radical militant action and which rejected the integration practised by King. They ridiculed statements by Martin Luther King like those in his famous speech in August 1963 at the Abraham Lincoln Memorial Monument in Washington: 'I have a dream that one day the sons of former slaves will sit down together with the sons of former slaveowners at the table of brotherhood in the red hills of Georgia.'

In keeping with Martin Luther King's vision, the struggle of the blacks was a commission given to them to restore dignity to the whole of humankind. Non-violence was the only possible means for this, but it was a means which was applied resolutely and from the deepest Christian motivation. He branded the generally passive church a 'social club with a thin veneer of religion' in which 'un-Christian Christians' come together who believe in the risen Christ but overlook the human Jesus. He formulated the following aspects as the basis for active non-violence.

1. Non-violent resistance is not a method for cowards – it does not mean a failure to resist injustice.

2. Non-violence does not destroy or humiliate the opponent.
3. Non-violence is an attack on the powers of evil, not on people who do evil.
4. Non-violence includes the readiness to endure humiliation without taking revenge and without hitting back.
5. One must not be drawn into violence either outwardly or inwardly.
6. Active non-violence come about in the conviction that the universe is on the side of justice.

Here King refers theologically to the Greek term *agape*, i.e. unselfish, active love, 'God's love which works in human hearts'. This kind of love is at work among those who profess non-violence.

In July 1964 Congress resolved to abolish racial discrimination. King, who that year was awarded the Nobel Peace Prize, now turned to a theme which had already fascinated him in his youth, namely poverty. He knew that he already had his greatest successes behind him and that it would become more difficult to bring about actual changes in this sphere: 'From the question of human dignity they will not move on to plans affecting the basic system of social and economic power. At this level the plans of the negroes extend beyond the race problem and are concerted with economic inequality wherever it is to be found.' A positive peace of the kind that King imagined would call for greater changes, for 'one of the ineradicable contradictions with which we have to do is that each person speaks of the struggle for peace, but that among those in power, in practice peace is nobody's business'. Martin Luther King was relieved of this task by his murder in Memphis. Therefore his family and also many observers always had their doubts about the truthfulness of the criminal investigation which attributes this murder to an individual.

Literature

Martin Luther King, *A Testament of Hope*, ed. J.M.Washington, San Francisco: Harper 1986.
S.B.Oates, *Let the Trumpet Sound*, London: Search Press 1982.

Máiread Maguire

To be created for love

In 1976 a car which went out of control killed two of her nephews and a niece. The driver, a member of the Irish Republican Army, had just been shot by British soldiers patrolling in the streets of Belfast. This death of the children changed Máiread Maguire's life dramatically. Together with Protestant women, the Irish Catholic organized peace marches in both Protestant and Catholic districts and founded the Peace People. Formerly on the staff of a firm in Northern Ireland and honorary director of the Legion of Mary – a Catholic group involved in social work – she soon became a public figure. The same year, with Betty Williams she received the Nobel Peace Prize.

'We achieve true freedom only when we have lost and let go of everything. Then we are really free to perform our task, which is to love and to be loved. I believe that then people can see that the human person represents the highest value in society,' Máiread Maguire declared. She added that through loss and crisis people have the opportunity to recognize how violent they themselves are. This insight is the presupposition for the capacity to see how one's opponents are bound up with one's own person and to recognize the necessity for non-violence.

Maguire sees the civil war in Northern Ireland as a crisis of identity in two opponents: the Catholic Republican rebel movement versus the British military; the efforts to detach Northern Ireland from the United Kingdom versus the aims of the Protestant loyalists. 'People kill in order to defend their identify, their Britishness or Irishness.' However, for Maguire reconciliation becomes possible only when humanity is recognized as the binding foundation and as an intrinsic value it precedes all religious and national identities which lead to segregation. But this is a learning process in the course of which people learn to let go and return to their true identity – to be created for love.

For Maguire this is not just a moral appeal; it is bound up with the need to create political institutions at a local level, for love is always closely linked with hatred, especially when political systems have organized violence. 'The will to love and the will to hate are the same love. What we must insist on in a world in which political power claims the right to murder is the will to love. We must do this even if it means our own death or – and this is even more difficult to imagine – the suffering and death of our nearest and dearest.'

She says that violence must be observed with 'the hard clarity of the diamond', and attacked in the real world. Here Máiread Maguire has always been involved in local and in small but effective steps. Initially she and other women organized lifts on prison visiting days for women of both religious communities who wanted to see their men, who had been imprisoned for politically motivated acts. The shared bus journey was followed by shared activities which slowly brought about trust among those involved.

In 1993 Maguire appealed to the IRA to lay down their arms and to continue their work with non-violent means. As the aim of achieving recognition and respect for the political visions of the Republican movement had already been achieved, Maguire called on the IRA now also to show in non-violent controversy the courage that they had shown in the armed struggle. In her letter to the IRA she indicates her belief in a non-violent and non-militarized society in Northern Ireland. A similar letter also went to the armed groups on the other side in the conflict

Máiread Maguire identified as one cause of the conflict the impossibility of the population of Northern Ireland sharing in decisions determining their own future. She felt that the current form of democracy was ordained from above, hierarchically structured, but without any real possibility of expressing itself on the urgent features of everyday life: the housing situation, the possibilities of work, or the problems of the environment. So the Peace People organized themselves in the various neighbourhoods into groups of about 3,000 people who discussed these topics. In this way the disadvantaged neighbourhoods could introduce their actual decisions into politics without having to fall in with nationalistic attitudes. The illusion of being represented through national or religious allegiance gave way to the possibility of being able to introduce their own ideas.

Breaking down fear is for Maguire one of the most important measures against violence. She concedes that she herself was afraid at the beginning of her public life. She was afraid, not so much that something could happen to her but that she could not deal with the expectations that were addressed to her. The mother of five children, she overcame this fear, and is committed not only to non-violent solutions in the Northern Ireland conflict but also to human and civil rights in other parts of the world as a presupposition for a lasting peace. Her support for the Burmese opposition politician Aung San Suu Kyi and the Nigerian writer and human rights activist Ken Saro-Wiwa, executed in 1995, is connected with this. After a journey to Burundi in 1995 she declared that the churches had failed in the face of ethnic conflicts. But the presupposition for this work is to bring about a change in oneself – and that, as Máiread Maguire remarks, is the most difficult task. The painful and humiliating recognition how far we are from truly non-violent action makes clear the fractures in ourselves on which we have to work. However, for her, reconciliation aimed at overcoming inner alienation is possible only with a spiritual attitude, the awareness of a divine presence. She sees the value of prayer not so much in a conversation with God as in the Spirit speaking the truth to men and women. For 'if our non-violence is rooted only in a form of enlightened self-interest, or proceeds from nothing but a highly cultivated sensitivity, or respectability, or a loveable character, then I fear that it will collapse when – as is certain – it comes up against great resistance or is threatened with immediate or violent death.'

Fellowship is needed for withstanding this challenge in the interest of survival; mutual support in the effort to be real peace-makers.

Literature

Marie-Pierre Bovy, Hildegard Goss-Mayr, Máiread Maguire and Sulak Sivarska, *Reconciliation: Reflections on the Occasion of the 75th Anniversary of the International Fellowship of Reconciliation*, Patterns in Reconciliation 1, Alkmaar: International Fellowship of Reconciliation 1994.

Dorothee Sölle

Worldly mystic of Protestantism

'We need another political spirituality. It is in the nature of violence that it helps us to get used to it and at the same time drives hope into exile. Before our eyes the memory of another life and images of it decay. Righteousness – as the most important name of God that the Jewish and Christian traditions have articulated – and its consequential action, solidarity, are dying in our land.'

Dorothee Sölle seems to have become more sceptical than she was at the beginning of her writing career, especially at the beginning of the 1970s, when she opposed the Vietnam war. At the time of the movement against stationing new nuclear missiles in Europe, when she suffered legal intimidation for her involvement in the blockades at the nuclear establishment at Mutlangen, she could still write:

How shall we recognize an angel
except by the fact that he gives courage where there was fear,
joy where once there was nothing but sorrow,
agreement where compulsion prevailed,
disarmament where terror threatened credibly?
Do not fear, the resistance is growing.

All her life she has lamented people's indifference, the personal and political apathy; she tries to rouse them and overcome the separation between mystical experience of God and active resistance. The thought of the theologian and writer and her political and social action belong together.

Dorothee Sölle was born in Cologne in 1929. She studied theology, philosophy and literature in Cologne, Freiburg and Göttingen. She finished her doctorate in 1959 and her habilitation in 1962. Then followed teaching in the USA and in Hamburg. Since 1960 Dorothee Sölle has been active as a writer. Her extraordinarily extensive writing focusses time and again on women, those without rights, the weak, and current issues of war and peace, justice and solidarity. In the face of the scandalous silence of the churches where they should have taken a stand, in the face of a piety which does not name those responsible, Sölle looks for a theological language which does justice to suffering. For her, the object of theological thought is peace in the sense of *shalom*, a peace which goes beyond the mere absence of visible direct violence.

Dorothee Sölle does not want once more to transform balances of power and unjust structures, economic relations and political truth, into religious or philosophical conceptuality: she calls for a sociological description of how things are. However, she wants to reflect on the situation with Christian faith in order 'to reclaim land from the sea of speechless death'. Around twenty-five years later Sölle describes her spirituality as mystical, but always related to social reality, free from esoteric modes which deny the world. 'Neither the church, which I experienced more as a stepmother, nor the spiritual adventure of a post-Enlightenment theology, has seduced me into a lifelong attempt to think about God. I am not professionally anchored, or even at home, in either of the two religious institutions of church and academic theology. It is the mystical element which will not let me go. To put it provisionally and simply, it is the love of God which I want to live out, understand and disseminate.'

Her actions have been consistent with this: her provocative visit to North Vietnam in 1962; her involvement in the non-violent demonstrations of the peace movement in the 1980s which have already been mentioned; her work as an observer at the elections in Nicaragua in 1984; her support of a shared left-wing list at the German Bundestag elections in 1990; and her opposition to the murderous racism in the Germany of the 1990s, both on the streets and in politics and bureaucracy.

Dorothee Sölle began to grapple with the dominant male-governed reality in her youth, when she discovered and analysed the extent of the Nazi crimes. 'The human suffering, seen as it actually was, destroys all innocence, all neutrality, all "It wasn't me, I could do nothing about it, I didn't want it." In the face of the suffering there is no third place beyond the victim and the executioner.'

Then she saw in Vietnam that the murderous contempt for human beings was not over. She was terrified at the political indifference, but also at her own inability to communicate and gain support against the war among those who were making political decisions in Germany. For Sölle, 'Vietnam continued the history of Auschwitz; that – as then – people did not see it with seeing eyes and did not hear it with hearing ears.'

In the world of the rich, God is also made a 'God of apathy' – a Christianity free of suffering has used the death of Christ theologically to guarantee a seamless course of exploitation in the doctrine that 'Christ has done enough for us so that our suffering is no longer necessary for the realization of salvation'. According to Sölle, the consequence is that prayer as a form of address to God is already a subversive act in industrial society, in which people find a language for expressing desires, pain and happiness.

But it is necessary to take seriously the way in which others suffer over social and political oppression and not dismiss it as alien suffering in order to put oneself in a position to bring about change: 'We can repress suffering . . . step by step and abolish it. But wherever we go we come up against limits which cannot be passed. Not only is death such a limit; there is also dulling and desensitizing, mutilation and wounding, which cannot be reversed. The only way to cross these barriers is to share the pain of the sufferers, not to leave them alone and make their cry louder.'

'God has no hands but ours,' Dorothee Sölle once wrote, quoting a famous mystic, and as a mystic she dares to think the thought that the Christian God does not only love human beings but also needs their active love. For the woman who also criticizes the peace movement because it lacks political spirituality and gets used to the structural violence of postmodern society, peaceful action is one of the prime tasks. In her book *I Shall not Get Used to Violence*, she writes provocatively that she is not non-violent. For in her view, the first step from a naïve rejection of violence and thus from violence itself is the recognition of being fettered to destruction by her own circumstances. The second is the certainty that violence can be interrupted. By saying a clear no to the compulsion to violence, say, through non-violent action, it is possible to 'tear the net for a moment, for a moment to sense the wind of freedom'.

Her goal is not an end to all conflicts but a temporary interruption of violence, like that which Jesus Christ experienced at his arrest. The basis for this is a strong self, a spiritual power which makes it possible to renounce violence and take the risk of approaching the conflict with non-violent means. This also entails that the means which are used to complete God's work do not themselves involve violence and thus do not contradict the aim of non-violence. In these thoughts Dorothee Sölle takes up the earliest Christian tradition, a continuation of the Pax Christi in the face of the state's Pax Romana, a peace achieved through military power and oppression and Franciscan models of the interruption of violence. It is her aim to resist the way in which today people get used to death.

Literature

Dorothee Sölle, *Suffering*, London: Darton, Longman and Todd 1972.

Dorothee Sölle, *Thinking about God*, London: SCM Press and Philadelphia: TPI 1990.

Dorothee Sölle, *Gewalt: Ich soll mich nicht gewöhne*, Düsseldorf: Patmos Verlag 1994.

Dorothee Sölle, *Mystik und Widerstand: du stilles Geschrei*, Hamburg: Verlag Hoffman und Campe 1997.

Desmond Tutu

Not partisan, but not neutral

'There are some remarkable people who believe that no one may
ever use violence, even against the most horrific crime. Such
absolute pacifists believe that the gospel of the cross forbids anyone taking up the sword, however just the cause may be. I admire
such people very much, but to my regret must confess that I am
made of less noble material.'

Bishop Desmond Tutu, who in 1984 was awarded the Nobel
Peace Prize for his non-violent opposition to the apartheid regime
in South Africa, and eleven years after the democratization of his
country was nominated Chairman of the Truth Commission,
showed great understanding about the armed war of the African
National Congress for the liberation of the black majority population. Long accused by the whites in power of demagogy, today he
works for the cohesion of the country and a reconciliation of the
different groups of the population.

Desmond Mpilo Tutu was born in the Transvaal in 1931, the
child of a Methodist family which went over to Anglicanism soon
after their move to Johannesburg. Like his father, at first he was a
teacher, but he resigned when apartheid laws which disadvantaged
blacks were enforced in the educational situation. Theological
studies followed, and at the age of thirty he was ordained priest by
the Anglican Church. On becoming bishop in the independent
mountain kingdom of Lesotho in 1976, his criticism of the government never fell silent. In 1978 he was appointed General Secretary
of the South African Council of Churches – as the press used to
say, 'the hot seat among church offices', in an 'arena where angels
fear to tread'. Here he had a forum from which he could call for a

boycott of the apartheid regime and condemn racial segregation. His church career did not interrupt this: in 1984 Tutu was made Anglican Bishop of Johannesburg; just two years later he became Archbishop of Capetown, i.e. supreme head of the Anglican Church in South Africa.

This physically small man, who twice had his passport withdrawn, sees himself as a tormenting spirit; he is characterized by directness and a sense of humour. Whereas even at the end of the 1980s Desmond Tutu was criticizing the US government for its silence on South African politics, his work shifted increasingly towards mediation and enabling negotiations with the banned African National Congress. At the beginning of 1987 he had a personal meeting with ANC representatives whom he saw being forced into the armed struggle by South African policies. He was sharply criticized by the government for this contact with 'terrorists'. But Tutu retorted that 'the morality of most whites to violence is both selective and directed towards their own ends'. In a situation in which what was legally right did not correspond to what was morally correct and the population was being oppressed by structural violence, it was 'necessary to obey God rather than human authorities'.

At the same time Tutu understands his church position as a political one. He gains authority and carries conviction by devoting himself wholly to questions of justice and truth, but keeps out of party politics and does not allow himself to be used politically. For some years he forbade the priests under him to become members of political parties, but in 1995 he campaigned for the broadest possible participation in elections. 'Committed theology cannot be neutral. It is a theology which is carried on with passion!' was one of his electoral slogans.

Although he admired the non-violent resistance of the black population to the policy of apartheid, for example through boycotts, and called on politicians internationally to support these efforts, Tutu also expressed doubts about the efficacy of non-

violence in the situation of the time. 'I am theologically conservative and traditional. The dominant attitude of my church on the
question of violence is this: all violence is bad – both the violence
of an unjust system like apartheid and the violence of those who
want to overthrow it. Therefore we have condemned necklacing
and car bombs as vigorously as the use of violence by the government or the security forces. However, that does not mean that the
dominant tradition of the church does not concede reluctantly
that in some situations violence is necessary.' Tutu refers to
Dietrich Bonhoeffer's involvement in the attempt on Hitler's life,
but warns that a lack of support for non-violent attempts could
lead to a civil war.

Tutu is fond of comparing the present situation after the abolition of the apartheid system in South Africa with the exodus of the
Israelites from Egypt: it is not a simple time, and doubts about the
process of reconciliation must be suppressed in the hope of overcoming the violence which is present in society. There is hope in
the belief that even people who have committed monstrous crimes
are capable of change. But reconciliation can be achieved only in
connection with truth and not through state ordinances, since
only the victims can forgive.

As Chairman of the Truth Commission, which is seeking to
clear up the crimes of the past, but after due confession on the part
of those investigated also holds out the prospect of an amnesty,
Tutu shows himself to be non-partisan. When the ruling ANC
wanted to exempt some members from a public hearing Tutu
threatened to resign: 'We are concerned to get to the truth in order
to heal this country.' Desmond Tutu does not believe that South
Africa has a patent recipe for peace, but he is confident that hope
could radiate from South Africa for people in regions of conflict
like Northern Ireland or Rwanda.

Literature

Shirley du Boulay, *Tutu: Archbishop without Frontiers,* London: Hodder 1996.

Desmond Tutu, *Rainbow People of God. South Africa's Victory over Apartheid,* ed. John Allen, New York: Doubleday 1994.

ISLAM

Giasuddin Ahmed

Revolution of hearts

His father did not want the sixteen-year old boy to live in the family home any more because he had criticized the imam of a mosque. However, his mother prevented the young Giasuddin Ahmed from being kicked out of the family. Some time previously, in the college hostel, he had encountered the works of Marx and Mao, and also friends who were in favour of the fight against the bourgeoisie and promised themselves the liberation of what was then East Pakistan.

East Pakistan, present-day Bangladesh, was until 1971 the eastern half of the state of Pakistan. At the partition of India in 1947 this Muslim part of Bengal had been given to Pakistan, but soon it was increasingly striving for independence. At the end of the 1960s Giasuddin Ahmed, who was born in 1952, became involved in discussions about social utopias which left a deep mark on him.

In 1970 he broke off the studies which he had just begun because the war of liberation against Pakistan had started. Giasuddin fled to India to join the independence movement there. For despite his dream of an independent Bangladesh, he was terrified by the brutality of the war and began to work as a volunteer in the refugee camps in Indian West Bengal. Here he was responsible for the distribution of essential rations and himself lived in extremely simple conditions. With only a sleeping mat and one piece of clothing he felt free and content. Before the end of the war of liberation the eighteen-year-old returned home, homesick for his mother. He crossed the frontier at great peril.

Hopelessness at that time dominated the thinking of many young people. 'At this time I was inspired by the Almighty. I gained inner strength. I began to persuade the young people around me to take their lives into their hands again. I devoted myself even more to my prayers. Then I understood that prayer in fact works.' This experience became the basis for Giasuddin's life-long commitment to peace. Acquired knowledge cannot help humanity out of its present crisis, and is even used for oppression and violations of human rights. In this situation it is necessary to strive for wisdom: 'I must know myself, I must know my creator and my fellow human beings.' Only when people become true representatives of Allah, of God, i.e. only when they identify with other people and practise characteristics like goodness, forgiveness and justice, will they be ready to act effectively against social and structural violence.

Nevertheless, after the foundation of the independent state of Bangladesh in 1972 Giasuddin continued his studies, completing them in 1975 with an MA in English literature. After that he worked for seventeen years at various schools as an English teacher. During his student years he became part of a Muslim group whose members – without separating from the other religious communities in Bangladesh – studied Islam, discussed their insights and tried to put them into practice in society. As a teacher he was asked by various organizations to speak on topics like Islam and non-violence. Giasuddin felt that he should study this question at greater length. In 1988, with members of other religions he founded the Sampreeti ('Friendship') organization and became its president.

For Giasuddin, social practice stands in the foreground: 'I personally do not believe that I have to defend my convictions. As a Muslim I believe that the practice of Islam is reflected in real life

in all spheres, and in collaboration with all men and women . . .'
Giasuddin thought that more and more books or the foundation
of organizations would only frustrate the youth, since at the time
there was a lack of practical action and the implementation of
spiritual ideals. Since 1992 he has devoted himself wholly to work
in the grass-roots organization Sampreeti.

Sampreeti organizes joint educational programmes of Muslims,
Buddhists, Christians and Hindus, and in this way attempts to
counter 'communal tendencies', i.e. violence between members
of different religious communities. But peace work would be
meaningless in the context of Bangladesh were it not combined
with economic programmes. Measures to create income should
make it possible for women in particular to play a greater part in
the economic life of the country. Sampreeti brings in religion,
which is deeply rooted in Southern Asia, to further people's
material and spiritual development. Giasuddin has said that he is
alienated by the fact that religious leaders misuse their knowledge
'out of an inability to understand, interpretation based on wrong
beliefs, or a lack of spirituality'. The sentencing of women in some
areas of Bangladesh is an example of this. Therefore further education in peace training and dialogues, to which it invites clergy,
teachers and village counsellors, is part of the organization's
programme.

Giasuddin's recommendations for a Muslim practice of non-
violence include the cultivation of the spiritual foundations of
peace work, the promotion of goodness, and the practice of sharing at the family level, along with organizing and educating
sympathetic people in society. In addition social commitment is
needed: 'Go to the poor. Live with them. Work at the grass roots.
Know the problems of the poor, help them to build up their lives;
encourage them and make them aware of their power.' Giasuddin
is convinced that if people are aroused at the grass roots, the intellectuals and rich will be moved to support the protection of
fundamental human rights and the preservation of justice.

Conviction is needed to be able to live out these principles.
Giasuddin quotes the Qur'an:

Good and evil deeds are not alike. Requite evil with good, and
he who is your enemy will become your dearest friend. But none
will attain this save those who endure with fortitude and are
greatly favoured by Allah' (*Surah* 41, 34–35).

Giasuddin thinks that someone who has achieved this is really
free, and that with this power, violence can be ended in a 'silent
but powerful revolution of the heart'. Even if this goal seems very
distant, Giasuddin is more hopeful today than at the time of the
Bengali war of liberation: 'Human action is not in vain. To seek
peace is to attain peace. Peace today is not realized everywhere, but
it is possible. There is light.'

Mohammed Arkoun

Critical humanist of Islam

'I speak of concrete things. I am not an intellectual in cloudcuckoo-
land, but want the rights of critical reason to be elevated to
politics.'

That is how Professor Mohammed Arkoun, born in Taourint-
Mimoun in the Great Kabylei region of Algeria in 1928, describes
himself after teaching in Europe for three decades. However,
because there is no such thing as the politics he desires, because
critical writings are not read in the Muslim world, and even in
Europe there is little interest in looking at Islam other than in the
current categories, he has constantly to fight for freedom.

From 1950 to 1965 Mohammed Arkoun studied in Oran and

Algiers, later at the Sorbonne in Paris. He gained his doctorate in
1969. In the course of his teaching and research activity in Lyons,
Paris, Los Angeles, Rome, Louvain, Princeton and Amsterdam he
worked both on the Islamic tradition and on problems of modern
Muslim societies. For Professor Arkoun, both these things go
together. To renew Muslim societies, he argues, it is necessary to
grapple with the classical texts of Islam using the methods of
modern linguistics and cultural anthropology. 'For the Muslims
of today do not know their own thought; they know nothing of
their own civilization in the important period between the seventh
and the thirteenth centuries, when Arabic thought formed the
spiritual and cultural framework of reference even for Europeans.'

Mohammed Arkoun sees the relationship between Europe and
the Muslim world stamped by colonialism to the present day.
Colonial rule has left deep traces in the Near East and in North
Africa, above all by the formation of nation states in which elites
rule who are not supported by the broad population and who
cannot even provide them with the security that it promises them.
Professor Arkoun therefore criticizes the model of the nation state
as inappropriate, especially for Mediterranean Muslim societies,
in which the development of a civil society has been interrupted by
colonialism. At the same time he criticizes the West, and especially
the European states which made agreements with the governments that came into being after the independence of these states
and artificially support them. Out of a concern for economic (oil)
and geopolitical (Israel) interests the West works with dictatorships which despise human rights, but takes no notice of
democratic events which take up the Islamic heritage of these
societies.

No wonder, then, that a predominantly young population in
North Africa or the Middle East sees Islam as a last resort. For
them Islam is the expression of a hope of participating in political
events despite the overwhelming power of Europe. This movement uses Islam predominantly as a source of political slogans,

without grappling with the theological or spiritual content of the religion. Islam becomes a mythology in that the time of its foundation is stylized as one of truth and justice. Neither those regimes supported by the West nor the West itself leave room to grapple critically with the values which from the primal period of Islam today have been associated with social activity.

This analysis of the present situation has made Mohammed Arkoun important for the development of non-violent thinking in Islam. His work, motivated by the desire to demonstrate ways of liberation, continually grapples with the question of violence and describes methods of understanding violence against the background of Islamic thought. This is because for Mohammed Arkoun, being human essentially involves conflicts and a will for power. The Qur'an, he argues, speaks an existential word, i.e. it reflects dealing with these realities, but also with hope as an 'existential human dimension'. For this reason, texts stand side by side which on the one hand attest a deeply pacifist attitude and on the other intolerable violence. From an anthropological perspective Arkoun regards this as a universal human problem, since 'violence always exists alongside the holy'.

Whereas Modern Europe has encouraged secularism and laicism – i.e. the separation of the religious sphere from politics – it is now necessary to practise a politics which cultivates religious values: 'Looking for meaning means incorporating the spiritual, inner values which shape people, which give the character of holiness to the person.' Here Mohammed Arkoun still sets great hopes on Europe, the place where freedom of opinion and critical discussion are in fact possible today. He says that Europe is responsible for re-opening the discussion, investigating why conflicts have developed between the Western and the Muslim worlds, and why humanism has failed.

Realistically, in present circumstances Mohammed Arkoun sees little possibility of liberating Muslim societies from European domination and indigenous dictatorships. Probably nothing will happen without a comprehensive revolution. For the governments above all see the civil society which is developing, and from which democratization could develop, as a threat.

Here, however, he is not just thinking of the liberation of Muslims. There is also an opportunity for Christian Europe in a broader public perception of the representatives of liberal Islam, e.g. in North Africa. 'There is such a Muslim humanism; it exists. Who talks about it? Who allows a voice to express it? So we could open up a new area of solidarity which would help us together to overcome the history of the next centuries.'

Literature

Mohammed Arkoun, *Islam, Europe and the West*, London: I.B. Tauris 1996.

Farid Esack

A voice of tolerance and dialogue

Farid Esack was sitting with a Christian friend in his room and discussing the political situation. It was one evening during the years in which he studied in Pakistan. The two of them had a visit from Haji Bhai Padia, the leader of Tablighi Jama, an international Muslim renewal movement particularly active in South Asia, to which Esack had felt drawn since his youth. To Esack's dismay, Bhai Padia invited Esack's guest, the committed Christian, to pronounce the Muslim confession of faith. Esack, for whom support for justice was and is decisive, came into conflict with the conservative world-view of his organization.

'Believers, if you help Allah, Allah will help you and make you strong' (*Surah* 47, 7). Throughout his difficult childhood in South Africa Farid Esack found support in this saying from the Qur'an and it was sufficient motivation for him. To support God in his just battle alongside the suffering population was Esack's way out of the oppression of the policy of apartheid. So already as a nine-year-old boy he joined Tablighi Jama and spent ten years in this organization. As for others in these circles, 'help Allah' meant 'help God's religion'. This view of the world, which came into being in a situation in which religion was an important factor among uprooted groups of the population who were struggling to survive, only became shaky for him with the key scene in Pakistan described above.

Farid Esack was born in 1958, the sixth son of a woman factory worker in Wynberg, South Africa. A single parent, she brought the children up alone. In 1961 the district in which the family lived was declared a 'white' area so they were forced to move to a coloured township in Cape Province. There Farid Esack grew up in great poverty and completed his schooling in a school run by Christians. In 1968 he was arrested by the South African police for the first time for taking part in protests. As a child, he helped in the building of a new mosque in the settlement, and this inspired him to his decision to move to Pakistan for eight years to study Islam.

The experience of being part of an oppressed minority, but also of a fellowship with a solidarity which transcended the limits of religious communities, had influenced Farid Esack before he left South Africa. In Pakistan, he then came into contact with Christian organizations which were tackling poverty in the outer suburbs of Karachi. He was particularly impressed by the commitment of a group of young Pakistani Christians which was called 'Breakthrough'; they challenged his own religious attitudes. He writes years later that exchanges with them contributed greatly to strengthening and sustaining his own faith as a Muslim – at a time when he was studying at the same college as some of those who later were to lead the Taliban in Afghanistan. However, many of the members of the Muslim student association to which Esack belonged were more an example to him of how complete identification does not bring certainty, of how faith touches a person deep down within.

Esack's own approach to Islam formed in this time: 'I believe that there is a way between dehumanizing fundamentalism and fossilized tradition. That is the way of a radical Islam which is committed to social justice, personal freedom and the search for the transcendent beyond all institutionalized religious and dogmatic constructions. It is an Islam which challenges us to investigate our belief in accordance with personal and social categories.' After his return to South Africa in 1982 as a Muslim theologian, he developed these ideas in discussions with others and in 1984 founded the organization 'Call of Islam', committed to the political expression of Islam with reference to liberation from apartheid, the equality of the sexes, environmental questions and religious pluralism. As co-ordinator of this organization he was involved in a series of networks which were working for the abolition of apartheid and had exchanges with other religious organizations. This interest in interfaith dialogue brought him into contact with the World Conference of the Religions for Peace, in which he has since been involved in a variety of national and international functions. Since 1990 he has deepened his scholarly knowledge with further study of Muslim and Christian theology in England and Germany. Nevertheless, he has not given up either his writing or his political activity – in liberated South Africa, Nelson Mandela nominated him Commissioner for Sexual Equality. For at a time when a great many Muslim young people are wondering about the relevance of their religion, Esack wants to strengthen the voices for tolerance and human rights.

Farid Esack calls the responsibility not to be silent about injustice *fard kifayah*, one of those Muslim duties which are imposed on a society, like prayers at a funeral. However, he is opposed to the separation of personal and social morality: 'We have learned that personal conviction of the good is the essential thing: if I am pious and live a life free of (immoral) actions, then everything around me will become good. The truth is that usually these actions are only outgrowths or consequences of a whole system of exploitation and injustice. Personal morality which is within this system, or which does not question the system and its champions, makes little sense.'

It is just as out of keeping with Islam quickly to break off relations with social groups which support the injustices in society. The Qur'an points out that in this case the character of the relationship must be changed, 'because we have the duty to fall in with them – to enter into critical argument'. However, there is no support here for a blind reaction which is stamped by those who act unjustly. Muslims have freedom of choice to determine their actions themselves, trusting in God, as the Prophet Muhammad showed after his failure in the city of Taif. Defeated though he was by his brutal expulsion by the citizens of Taif, he took responsibility for his own feelings and guided his further behaviour by other criteria. Esack refers to this episode from the life of the Prophet and emphasizes the freedom of individuals to assume social responsibility.

To be able to achieve that – Esack keeps stressing his own imperfection in the face of these claims – it is necessary to maintain access to oneself, to one's own healing powers, like the Prophet, who went into solitude for long periods to be alone with himself and God so that he did not destroy himself. Then it is possible to overcome the separation of people from one another in a world which is so stamped by our capitalism and science, and also by our inability to perceive and communicate our own feelings and those of others, so that we can listen where support is necessary. For Esack emphasizes that mutual solidarity instead of self-righteous judgment is necessary to preserve one's own integrity as a human being.

Literature

Farid Esack, *Qur'an, Liberation and Pluralism: An Islamic Perspective of Inter-Religious Solidarity against Oppression*, Oxford: One World 1997.

Farid Esack, 'Esack's Corner', regular column in *As-Salamu 'Alaykum*, Nyack, NY: Muslim Peace Fellowship, November 1995–1998.

Abdul Ghaffar Khan

A servant of God

'I vow in honesty and truthfulness to become a true servant of God. I will sacrifice my possessions, my life and my prosperity for the freedom of my nation and my people. I will never take part in division, hatred or envy in my people and will stand on the side of the oppressed against the oppressor. I will never become a member of any other rival organization, nor will I serve in an army. I will always obey all legitimate commands of my superior. I will live in accord with the principles of non-violence. I will serve all God's creatures equally, and it will be my goal to attain freedom for my land and my religion. I will always be concerned to do what is right and good. I will never require any reward for my service. My whole effort will be to please God, not ostentation or profit.'

Every member of the so-called Khudai Khidmatgar, the 'Servants of God', had subscribed to this oath. The organizer of the group which acted against the British colonial government in North-West India in the 1930s was the Muslim Pathan Abdul Ghaffar Khan.

Abdul Ghaffar Khan was born in 1890, a member of the Pathan

tribe which inhabited a large part of Afghanistan and the North-West Province of British India. Whereas as early as 1919 neighbouring Afghanistan, after internal unification, became independent, the Pathans remained part of the strategically important North-West Province. Abdul Ghaffar Khan's older brother was involved in the politics of the independence movement at a very early stage, but he himself went other ways. Even as a youth he decided to serve God through social reforms and educational work. In 1929 he founded Khudai Khidmatgar, as the subsidiary organization of a local political party which had already existed since 1926. Khudai Khidmatgar became increasingly important, though in subsequent years the Khan brothers turned to the politics of the Indian National Congress.

When it became known that a group using non-violent means had formed among the Muslim Pathans there was amazement, and not just among the British. The tribes of the frontier region and particularly the Pathans were known throughout India for their wildness and lack of restraint. They were regarded as always armed, in principle prepared for acts of violence and virtually uncontrollable. Certainly there were also some Muslims in Mahatma Gandhi's non-violent movement, but so far a non-violent movement based on Islam was unknown. In the Pathan liberation movement which now formed, its members committed themselves to pursue non-violence not only as a political tactic but as a principle of life. Here Abdul Ghaffar Khan made quite successful use of cultural ideals of bravery and sacrifice to motivate the members of the group. He responded to criticism in a conversation with a Muslim: 'He criticized me fiercely and said that I was undermining the spirit of Islam by preaching non-violence to the Pathans. I told him that he did not know what he was saying and that he would not say it had he seen with his own eyes the miraculous transformation that the idea of non-violence had brought about among the Pathans and how it had given them a new vision of national solidarity. I quoted paragraphs and verses from the Qur'an to demonstrate the great importance that Islam attaches to peace. It is its core. I went on to show him that the greatest personalities in Muslim history have been known more for their deprivations and their renunciation than for their brutality.'

Abdul Ghaffar Khan, who because of his non-violent organization was also called the 'Gandhi of the Frontier', based his commitment to the well-being of all creatures and freedom of the oppressed – like the oath and name of the organization – on a concern to please and serve God. This is the expression of a mystical attitude of Islam which has been formulated time and again in Central Asia and has been carried around on the Indian sub-continent by itinerant preachers: act in order to please God. An ascetic lifestyle rich in deprivation is also part of the cultural heritage of the mystical poets and preachers of the region.

The Khudai Khidmatgar, also called 'Red Shirts', were organized hierarchically. However, what is striking about their oath is the reservation that while they would obey the orders of their superiors, they would obey only the legitimate orders. A year after its foundation the organization already had 5,000 members. In 1930 Gandhi began what was probably his most important campaign, the Salt March, with which by unmasking unjust colonial laws he wanted to persuade the British to agree to the political self-determination of India. In parallel to this there were demonstrations against alcohol shops and strikes. The movement found a particularly large amount of support in the Pathan provincial capital of Peshawar. Abdul Ghaffar Khan organized the resistance with the Red Shirts, spoke indefatigably at meetings and finally was arrested in the second half of April.

The arrest of Badshah Khan, as Abdul Ghaffar was called by friends, unleashed a storm of indignation and further demonstrations which the colonial troops wanted to put an end to with violence. Pathan women took part in the demonstrations and opposed the soldiers. On 23 April 1930 elite regiments manned by

Indian soldiers refused to obey the orders of the colonial administration to continue to shoot at the unarmed crowd – and were withdrawn. The Khudai Khidmatgar took over rule in Peshawar and within a few days established a parallel administration with its own system of taxation. The brief experience of freedom lasted nine days – then a great wave of repression began under white troops which had hastily been brought in. Abdul Ghaffar Khan remained in prison for a long time and even after his release was not allowed to return to his own region. In 1957 Gandhi wrote in the preface to a biography of the Pathan freedom fighter: 'Mr Abdul Ghaffar Khan seems to be a real fakir. I see this character trait in the letter which he wrote from prison. From day to day his self-denial became greater and the thought of God in his heart deeper.'

Gandhi, who wanted to visit the North-West Province, received a permit to do so only in 1938. At that time the Kudai Khidmatgar had grown, above all through local support, to almost 100,000 members. Accordingly, the organization also pressed to an increasing degree for social reforms. This gave the Khudai Khidmatgar a strong basis for supporting the Indian National Congress in its negotiations for the unity of India. There was resistance to the North-West Province becoming part of Pakistan on the division of the sub-continent.

Abdul Ghaffar Khan still took part in demonstrations to bring peace to the land even in the months before the independence of India, when at the beginning of 1947 unrest between Hindus and Muslims claimed human lives in many regions of India. There were reports from Bihar and Bengal, where he went on foot from village to village with Gandhi and other activists of the non-violent movement, that Abdul Ghaffar Khan was impressive both in his physical stature and in his authenticity. He reminded the politicians of the Muslim League, a party above all of Muslim land owners who under the leadership of M. A. Jinnah fought for and were able to establish an independent Pakistan against the Indian

National Congress, that it was their duty as Muslims to disseminate tolerance. He wrote to Gandhi that he was beginning to abhor
politics if hatred was disseminated in the name of religion. In
Patna, the capital of Bihar, he said at an interfaith meeting: 'India
today seems like an inferno of madness. My heart weeps when I see
how we are setting fire to our own houses. Today I see darkness
rule over India and my eyes turn vainly everywhere in an attempt
to see light.'

After the division of the sub-continent into India and Pakistan,
Abdul Ghaffar Khan quickly lost his paramount political significance. The Khudai Khidmatgar were persecuted by the Pakistani
government and Abdul Ghaffar Khan, who was accused of collaboration with Indians and Hindus, had to spend another fifteen
years in prison. He died on 21 January 1988 and at his own wish was
buried in Afghanistan.

Literature

Joan V. Bondurant, *The Conquest of Violence: The Gandhian
    Philosophy of Conflict*, Princeton, NJ: Princeton University
    Press 1958.
Naryan Desai, *The Fire and the Rose*, Ahmedabad: Navajivan
    Publishing House 1995.
Robert C.Johansen, 'Radical Islam and Non Violence: A Case
    Study of Religious Empowerment and Constraint Among
    Pashtus', *Journal of Peace Research* 34 no.1, 1997, 53–71.
Pyarelal, *Mahatma Gandhi. The Last Phase, Vol. I, Book Two*,
    Ahmedabad: Navajivan Publishing House 1995.

Fatima Mernissi

Overcoming limits

'The imagination can no longer be forbidden the freedom to reflect on or imagine something, since it is the place of inventions, the source of wealth in the electronic age. It is here that the great cultural debates which the Muslims are called on to accept and above all to resolve must take place.' Fatima Mernissi has opened this cultural debate with her writings, her lectures and above all her constant readiness to engage in dialogue – both in Europe and in her homeland, Morocco. That has made her the best-known woman scientist, writer and feminist in North Africa.

Fatima Mernissi was born in 1940 into a prosperous middle-class family which lived in the old city, the Medina of the Moroccan royal city of Fez. There she grew up in the harem of the extended family, the closed space for women and children – an experience which she describes in her book *The Harem Within*. It has influenced her thought to the present day. Her father was close to the nationalist movement which wanted to secure the independence of Morocco from France and Spain. So in her family, polygamy and slavery belonged to the past, and education was held up as an ideal. Fatima Mernissi first went to a convent school, but then she attended an ordinary school and later was one of the first thirty-seven women in the country to go to the University of Rabat; she then went on to Paris and Massachusetts. Today she is Professor of Sociology in Rabat and since 1973 has been adviser to UNESCO on the situation of Muslim women.

Models of her childhood include S'heherazade, the story-telling princess from the *Thousand and One Nights*. 'In our part of the world S'heherazade is regarded as a bold heroine, and she is one of our few mythical female figures. S'heherazade is a great strategist and compelling thinker, who uses her psychological knowledge of people to inspire them and encourage them.' Wit, imagination and narrative skill are also among the characteristics which mark out Fatima Mernissi and with which she seeks to fight for the rights of women and demonstrate models for the survival of Arab societies.

The limits of the family harem, and the cultural and political significance of limits generally, have occupied Fatima Mernissi from her childhood. Certainly the views of the women with whom she was surrounded as an adolescent girl were contradictory where the harem was concerned. But her mother and a divorced aunt provided models for resistance against this institution. For Fatima Mernissi, it was the veil which in her youth women in cities in Morocco had slowly began to discard that was the most potent symbol. In opposition to an Islamic tradition which emphasizes the dignity and political status of the woman by the wearing of a veil, she sees the modern pressure to wear the veil as the effort of a system shaken with crises to make women invisible and silence them.

However, Fatima Mernissi does not see veils at work only in the Arab world. The most famous example for her was the Berlin Wall, the manifest expression of the 'Iron Curtain' – and in Arabic 'curtain' is the same word as 'veil'. In her view, the exclusion of refugees along with racist thinking in Germany are similar phenomena of setting limits. These limits are erected for one's own protection, to guarantee stability and security.

Fatima Mernissi's analysis is that with the fall of the Berlin Wall and the end of the socialist dictatorships in Eastern Europe, many people hoped that the justification of political violence would come to an end and a new age of democratization would dawn. But only a few months later these hopes were shattered by the Gulf War, justified by the authority which was most associated with the values of freedom and self-determination, the United Nations.

People who had been restricted from exercising their freedom by dictatorships recognized that, despite professions to the contrary in support of democracy, the West would continue to collaborate with the undemocratic regimes of the Middle East and support them. The limits of freedom had once again been drawn more tightly. Especially the Arab women began to feel this.

Mernissi thinks that in the wake of the 1991 Gulf War new legitimacy was given to weak and ineffective systems which repress women and minorities and prevent the development of a civil society. But 'by veiling conflicts, they cut themselves off from the roots of vitality and creativity'. Here Fatima Mernissi sees it as her task to demonstrate alternatives.

The word and dialogue are important instruments for her here. Even as a child she experimented with words in order to 'turn them round seven times in the mouth'. As a scholar who leaves her study and tries to talk with people in the market or at their businesses, she rediscovers apparently familiar concepts. Instead of following interpretations of the Qur'an and the Hadith (the tradition from the life of the Prophet Muhammad) which serve to maintain power, she looked for the context of the revelations, for their deeper meaning in the production of justice, and in so doing gave life to a method which was already developed in the heyday of Muslim societies, but was subsequently suppressed. If revelations are interpreted in terms of their historical background, they take on meaning which extends far beyond their wording. Her way of investigating the Islamic tradition and its liberating meaning, and of gaining motivation from this to overcome problems of the present, has made Fatima Mernissi's thinking a model far beyond the feminist movement.

She sees Islam as a dynamic religion, which seeks to produce a balance in the tension between individual freedom and social security. Here the individual's passion and moods, in a wider sense the unrestrained interest of the individual, are opposed to the interest of society. But in Islam social peace is shaped by *rahma*, by mercy, sensibility and tenderness, i.e. by mutual responsibility. The fear that this quality is being lost in the post-colonial societies of the Middle East as a result of economic and political dependence is leading many people wrongly to want to limit individual freedoms. Fatima Mernissi calls on the political elites of these countries to overcome their anxiety and allow limits to be exceeded.

Here those who are most affected, the women, are her main concern. 'They are ready for the crusade, they have always been aware that the future lies in the destruction of the limit, that the individual is born to be respected, that difference is enriching.' She instructs women who in Moroccan society are still largely condemned to silence, in creative writing, as in the writers' workshop Femme Maghreb 2002 which she inspired. Or she organizes computer networking. In Rabat she has founded an emergency centre for women who have become victims of violence, and she is co-initiator of an independent human rights commission.

But Fatima Mernissi also names the bosses in Western governments and banks who are responsible for the continuing existence of regimes which scorn human rights: 'The West has very fine ideas, and now it has the occasion to show us that it is really more advanced and ethical than the rest of humankind.' The future of Arab societies depends on whether Eastern and Western states take responsibility for democratization and social equality. To have a vision, a dream, is a presupposition of liberation – Fatima Mernissi already learned this in the harem of her childhood.

Literature

Fatima Mernissi, *The Harem Within*, London and New York: Bantam Books 1995.

Fatima Mernissi, *Islam and Democracy: Fear of the Modern World*, Oxford: Polity Press 1993.

Fatima Mernissi, *Women and Islam: An Historical and Theological Memory*, Oxford: Blackwell 1991.

HINDUISM

Sunderlal Bahugana

Environmental activist, barefoot journalist and itinerant sage

'We are constantly being told that the poor people are ruining the forests by extending the fields and using up all the wood. Certainly they are doing that, but where are they to go, and what are they to eat? In the end, they too were born on this earth. But how little are their needs by comparison with those great industries, most of which do not manufacture products for human survival, absolutely necessary products, but luxury objects.'

This quotation describes Sunderlal Bahugana's concern and the area in which he is active. Together with the social worker Chandi Prasad Bhatt and the women of the mountain villages who supported them, above all in the 1970s and 1980s Bahugana gained recognition in India and internationally through the Chipko movement. It fights to protect the forests of the Himalayas against unlimited over-exploitation and has been able to bring about changes in the laws which are meant to regulate the economic use of the mountain forests.

Sunderlal Bahugana was born into a Brahman family in 1927, the son of a forestry official and farmer. His parents lived in a village in the district of Tehri-Garhwal in the north Indian Himalayan region of Uttarakhand. Bahugana was active as a follower of Gandhi in the independence movement as early as 1940. He soon began to campaign for the independence of India through his journalistic work. His capacity to describe quickly and in an easily understandable way the concerns of the movements in which he himself was engaged, and his researches, which continually also took him into remote regions, once earned him the title of 'barefoot journalist' – probably based on the barefoot doctors of revolutionary China.

In 1948 he met Jayaprakash Narayan (see pp. 87–91), whom he joined in the 1950s in connection with the land-gift campaigns (see p. 80). In 1956 he married Vimala, who was likewise active with Jayaprakash Narayan. Both returned to Uttarakhand and founded the Navajivan ashram (ashram for new life), in which they taught children from the neighbouring mountain villages and from which they began their work of social reconstruction. They carried the campaigns of the Gandhi movement for village autonomy into the mountains and there campaigned against the uncontrolled sale of alcohol.

When after the war between India and China in 1962 more work was done on developing the communication network on the frontier, the natural wealth of Uttarakhand was also opened up to the industry of the plain. The attack on the mountain forests very soon had its first effects on the ecological balance of the region and further areas of north India: in the rainy season deforested hill-sides collapsed into the rivers, whose beds rose, in turn causing devastating and catastrophic inundation. The destruction of the forests which provided springs and building materials, safeguarded the presence of sources of water and regenerated the earth, removed the basis of village existence. This had a particular impact on the women, who had to walk further and further for water and wood. So it was not surprising that first of all the women became restless and organized themselves against the stripping of the forests. The Chipko movement came into being (see below, p. 137). Sunderlal Bahugana gave it a voice in the cities and political centres abroad.

In 1974 Bahugana went on hunger strike in order to stop the annual auctions of forestry rights to private tenants, but at the same time he supported the forestry workers. He went on another fast in 1977 'to arouse the power of local workers'. In his speech connected with the fast, which was entitled 'The Forestry Workers – Heralds of New Life in the Mountains', he compared the workers with the mythological heroes Rama and Lakshman: 'Forestry workers, saws, axes and transport for trees are your bows and arrows. Come equipped with them, so that the demon of poverty and employment is killed.' At that time Bahuguna regarded the formation of co-operatives of forestry workers and an abolition of the system of contractors, which gave the rights to fell trees in an area to a contractor who hired forestry workers, as demands which, if fulfilled, would also solve the problems of protecting the forest.

Only a short time later he changed his attitude in view of the ecological significance of the forests for the whole of North India and opposed any commercial exploitation of the forest, including the economic use of it by local small industries. Between 1981 and 1983 he argued this view on long journeys by foot through Uttarakhand and also throughout the Indian Himalayan region from Kashmir in the west to Kohima in the east. At the same time these journeys served to attract the attention of the media, to disseminate the ideas of the movement in the mountain villages, and to allow the feedback of experiences from the local situation. Bahugana saw himself throughout as standing in the tradition of old Indian sages since Buddha, who disseminated their teachings on foot.

On such occasions Bahugana passed on the message to the population by pamphlets, but above all by songs and poems in the vernacular. In so doing he made use of a language which took up the myths and epics long known in India and which emphasized the significance of the forest for Indian culture. For example, he used the image of the wish-tree which fulfils all petitions, which came into being at creation and promises abundance, wealth and happiness, to make clear the paramount importance of trees for the economy of the mountain regions.

In addition to speaking in symbols he finds clear analytical words: 'Chipko is a rebellion against the extermination of nature and an attempt to restore the values of the forest culture by making spirituality the guideline for science and technology in order to benefit all living beings.' In this century reflection on India as a forest culture, as distinct from a city or village culture, has been inspired by the Bengali Nobel prize-winner Rabindranath Tagore. In this connection Sunderlal Bahugana stated the aim of doing away with the separation between the object and subject world – the environment and human beings – as being a cause of destruction: 'The Chipko movement is the attempt to make the harmony of self-knowledge and science an element of human lifestyle in the battle for survival.'

That is why Sunderlal Bahugana's poetic protest is increasingly directed against a model of development based on the rising production of commodities, which results in the unrestricted exploitation of resources important for life, in order to satisfy the needs of a luxury culture. Here he continued his protest against the destruction of the environment in the Himalayas and supported the non-violent movement against the great dam project in Tehri. In 1989 he was awarded the alternative Nobel Prize.

Literature

Hagen Berndt, *Rettet die Bäume in Himalaya*, Berlin: Quorum Verlag 1987.

Vinoba Bhave

Bringing the holy into politics

'I call myself a teacher, and I am never more content than when I can devote myself to study and teaching. It is such a peaceful and satisfying way of life that I would probably have lived to be one hundred if I kept to it. But I had to give it up and go public, because India is in danger.'

In the middle of 1948, a few months after the violent death of Gandhi, the members of the organization which he had founded met to unite and reorientate themselves. There was great perplexity among many of Gandhi's followers about how work for justice could be continued in an India which had become independent. Only three years later, when Vinoba Bhave went public with the *bhudan*, i.e. land-gift, campaign, could these be overcome. Vinoba Bhave had identified the concern which had fascinated the non-violent movement of India for a decade, the question of land which could give it direction.

Vinoba Bhave was born in 1895 in Gagoda, in the state of Maharashtra, but because his father changed status soon moved to Baroda, where he received his school education. At the age of ten, he decided to devote his life to spiritual goals and not to marry. At a very early stage he was impressed by the biographies of ancient Indian sages, especially those of Buddha, the mystic Ramdas and the philosopher Shankaracarya, who in the prime of life left house and family to devote themselves to the spiritual life. Very much to the sorrow of his mother, who supported his interest in religious literature, one day Vinoba burnt his testimonials, as he never wanted to apply for a job.

He made his dream of studying classical Sanskrit and the literature written in it come true in 1916, when he went to Varanasi (Benares). Later he wrote that he chose Varanasi out of the three places which attracted him because he could reach the others easily from there: the other two were the Himalayas, in India the symbol of the place where ascetics and sages lived, and Bengal, which was known for its revolutionary movements. However, when Vinoba arrived in Varanasi he heard there with great interest of a provocative speech which Gandhi had given a few weeks earlier, having just returned from South Africa. Vinoba entered into correspondence with Gandhi and finally visited him in his ashram in Ahmedabad, after Gandhi had admonished him that inner clarity would not be attained through words, but only in life.

Vinoba, whom Gandhi called Vinayak, a pet form of his name, stayed at Gandhi's ashram and with great dedication performed all the tasks imposed on him. In a letter to Vinoba's father, who would have preferred him to study French and engineering, Gandhi wrote: 'Your Vinoba is with me. Already at so young an age your son has undergone a development in his mental acuity and inner freedom of the kind that I was able to achieve only after many years.'

But the very next year the young man asked for a year's leave, in order to finish his literary studies and have time for toughening himself up physically. Gandhi referred to this time in 1940 when he explained why he had chosen Vinoba as the first 'individual *satyagrahi*', the one who offers civil disobedience. 'He entered the ashram almost immediately it was founded . . . In order to prepare himself better, he took a year's leave to study Sanskrit again. At precisely the hour when he had left the ashram a year previously, he returned . . . He took part in all the simple work in the ashram, from sweeping the paths to cooking. Although he had a marvellous memory and by nature is a student, he devoted the bulk of his time to spinning and perfected his skills in an unprecedented way. His basic assumption is that spinning generally is the central activity which will do away with rural poverty . . . He has removed any trace of untouchability from his heart . . . Like all our fellow workers, he believes that quiet constructive work with civil disobedience in the background is more effective than the political stage, which is already heavily populated. He believes that non-violent resistance is impossible without deeply being convinced of the importance of constructive work and practising it.'

For Vinoba, who devoted at least an hour a day to the study above all of religious literature, but also of historical and economic political texts, and who to an advanced age learned more than ten Indian, Asian and European languages, the practical activities prescribed by Gandhi were a contribution to perfecting himself spiritually. Interrupted by several stays in prison for taking parts in actions of civil disobedience which Gandhi had asked him to engage in ('For me your call is a command like the call of death'), Vinoba did construction work for most of 1921 to 1951 in the Wardha district of Central India. He described himself as a worker in cleansing activities, agricultural work and other occupations which were regarded as socially inferior. At the same time he practised inactivity in the spiritual sense, as one who has inwardly detached himself from the fruits of his work and thus has attained a higher freedom. His commentary on the Bhagavadgita, certainly the most influential Hindu text in the twentieth century, describes this goal and the way to it in an impressive way. The respect that Vinoba gained among the Indian population lay in his capacity to work out the meaning of traditional religious concepts for present-day problems with insight, humour and convincing authenticity, and to show their importance for the present. He restored the holy, for which a deep longing lives on in Indian society, to the everyday life of men and women and to politics.

In April 1951 Vinoba went through the villages of Telengan, a region in the present state of Andhra Pradesh, on the way to a conference. The police and army had just put down Communist-led unrest there. Previously the landless under the leadership of the Communist party had violently appropriated a series of estates and had redistributed the land. Vinoba saw the events in Telengan as a challenge to his notions of non-violence. He attempted to communicate to the people that no part of society can permanently live in an atmosphere of fear and destruction. The first reaction to this thesis, which on the surface supported an unjust system, was scepticism, but then success proved Vinoba right: a landowner gave him land to distribute to those without any.

Thus began the *bhudan* campaigns, for which Vinoba – fulfilling a vow – together with others went throughout India on foot. He sought to be accepted by the landowners as their sixth son in order to get a corresponding share of land. In connection with the land-gift campaign, in 1957 Vinoba Bhave founded the Shanti Sena ('peace army'), which was meant to create peace by non-violent means in regions of unrest (see 164f.). Some years later the *bhudan* campaign, along with the *gramdan* ('village-gift') movement, developed into a programme that combined elements of the collective regulation of production with the creation of basic democratic institutions which made decisions at village level on the principle of consensus. With the *bhudan* and *gramdan* campaigns Vinoba had set up creative instruments which moved India towards creating new forms of self-organization. However, after only two decades they lost their dynamic. Granted, by 1970 almost 100,000 villages in India had subscribed to the *gramdan* obligations, and even when infertile or unusable land had been subtracted, increasingly more was being distributed than through state land reforms. But in many places it was proving that this had brought about no real changes to the power structures. Vinoba's aim had been harmonious relations in the village – the notion of class warfare was incompatible with this. He expected nothing from the state and exclusively insisted on changes from below. Here, however, he ignored processes like centralized industrialization even of the agricultural economy, the constant advance of the state apparatus, and the corruption of the administration, which put the successes of the movement in question.

Vinoba recognized that the peak of his social responsibility had passed. From 1966 on he clearly put in the background commitment to the coarser – the political – things, in favour of the 'fine things', i.e. spiritual development. His year of silence from 1 December 1974 to December 1975 fell precisely at the time when Prime Minister Indira Gandhi proclaimed the state of emergency and had many of the opposition imprisoned, particularly those from the non-violent movement. Many Gandhians subsequently condemned him for not having criticized Indira Gandhi's policy as others had done.

Vinoba increasingly retreated into his ashram in Pauna, very near to Wardha. A few days after surviving a heart attack, he died there on 15 November 1982. Like an Indian saint who has done his duty in the world, his refusal to take water, food and medicine hastened his end. His understanding of himself is reflected in the words, 'I am a person of quite another world. My world is pure. My claim is that I have love. I continually experience this love. I have no doctrines, I have ideas.'

Literature

Vinoba Bhave, *Moved by Love: The Memoirs of Vinoba Bhave*, Totnes, Devon: Green Books 1994.

Mahatma Gandhi

'My experiments in the political sphere are now known not only in India but to some degree throughout the "civilized world". For me they are not of much value, and the title Mahatma which I have gained through them therefore even less. This title has often pained me; I cannot recall any moment at which it would have flattered me. However, I like to report my experiments in the spiritual sphere which only I know. For from them I have drawn the strength which makes possible my political work. If these experiments are really spiritual, there can be no room for self-praise. They can only contribute to my humility. The more I reflect on my past, the more I sense my limitations.'

Mahatma Gandhi wrote this comment in the introduction to his autobiography. He was always convinced that what is possible for one person could be done by everyone else. These remarks should not be dismissed as the modesty of a great man who was conscious of his greatness – they provide an approach to Gandhi's thinking. The title of his autobiography, which is characterized by great openness, is *Experiments with the Truth*. It explains the character of his action and his decisions, which were not always to be understood as political tactics, against another, spiritual, background.

Mohandas Karamchand Gandhi was born on 2 October 1869 in Porbandar in the present state of Gujarat. His father Karamchand had not had much formal education, but he was a senior administrative official in various small principalities. He was known for his incorruptibility, his impartiality and his civil courage. Gandhi's mother Putlibai impressed her son with her deep religious sense, he once even said 'holiness'. She was intelligent and well informed on political matters. The discussions which his father had with members of different religious communities in Gujarat interested the adolescent and increased his respect for other religious views. However, all in all, Gandhi wrote later, in his youth he did not have any living faith in God but tended rather towards atheism.

After he had been married at the age of thirteen to Kasturba, who was the same age, this marriage claimed the bulk of his attention, especially sexual attention. When three years later his father, for whose care he had constantly been responsible, died, he had been with Kasturba. This filled him with deep shame and became a key experience which led him to reflect all his life on sexuality and other bodily joys (e.g. tasty food). Later he arrived at the radical view that these bodily pleasures would divert him from his real task, namely service of God, which manifests itself in service of fellow human beings. Gandhi understood the Brahmacharya vows of sexual continence which he took in 1906 and maintained until the end of his life as an attempt to control all the senses for the struggle for Brahman, for God, for the truth: 'If my non-violence is really to be infectious, I must achieve greater control over my thoughts.'

In his youth Gandhi also made his first experiments with eating meat. His family belonged to the Hindu community of the Vaishnavas, who are strict vegetarians. An older school friend persuaded the young Gandhi secretly to eat meat. At first he did not like the taste, but he had become convinced that eating meat, as practised by the English, would also make Indian society stronger, and he felt obliged to join in this reform. However, he ended the experiment because in engaging in it he had to lie to his mother so as not to hurt her. Still, only during his years of study in England did he make a deliberate decision to be a vegetarian. For Gandhi, the quest for truth – the leitmotif of his life – excluded lies and later also secrecy. Even as a young man he was convinced that an open and radical confession of his own mistakes, a readiness to expose himself to criticism for his behaviour, i.e. to take responsibility for himself and his actions, was an indispensable step towards cleansing and reconciliation. In his public life Gandhi thus amazed his companions in the political struggle, to whom this openness even towards the British colonial administration sometimes seemed clumsy tactics.

In the course of his three-year study of law in London Gandhi came into contact with members of the Theosophical Society and had the opportunity to grapple with critical ideas from the end of the nineteenth century and the main texts of the world religions – especially the Hindu Bhagavadgita, the teaching of the Buddha and the Sermon on the Mount. After two years of unsuccessful attempts to establish himself as an advocate in his homeland of Gujarat and in Bombay, he accepted the offer to represent an

Indian businessman in South Africa in a law case. Only a few days after his arrival, although he had a valid ticket, because he refused to leave the compartment in the train reserved for whites, he was violently dumped on the platform and so had his first experience of racial segregation.

Gandhi later described this situation and his resolve not to evade the conflict but to oppose injustice in principle as being the hour of birth of his most important concept, *satyagraha*: 'Its original meaning is holding firm to the truth, and therefore the power of truth. I have also called it the power of love or the power of the soul. At the earliest stage In the application of *satyagraha* I discovered that the quest for truth does not allow one to do violence to one's opponent but that he must be diverted from his error with patience and sympathy . . . So it came about that the doctrine means the defence of the truth, not by inflicting suffering on an opponent but by suffering oneself.'

For Gandhi, *satyagraha* and non-violence were two closely interwoven concepts. He recognized that human life is always entangled in violence and that therefore the profession of non-violence means being led by empathy and love to work for liberation from this relationship of violence. He laid down the following 'axioms' for non-violence: '1. Non-violence includes the most human purging of the self possible. 2. For every person, the strength of his non-violence corresponds precisely to his capacity – not his will – to use violence. 3. Non-violence is without exception superior to violence; that means that the power available to a non-violent person is always greater than what he would possess if he applied violence. 4. In non-violence there is nothing like a defeat. The aim of violence is in any case defeat. 5. The ultimate aim of non-violence is in any case victory – if such a concept can be applied in the case of non-violence. In reality, where there is no concept of defeat, there is also no concept of victory.'

After Gandhi had returned to India in 1915, by now famous as a result of his political work in South Africa (he had been given the additional name Mahatma – one who has a great soul – by Rabindranath Tagore), he joined the independence movement. He soon had an opportunity to apply his experiences with *satyagraha* on the Indian continent on behalf of the indigo farmers, who had been impoverished by excessive rents. He was arrested, put on trial for causing unrest, and acquitted, although he declared himself guilty. In the years following Gandhi soon managed to create a mass base for the independence movement and to unite it. However, when in 1919 a campaign of civil disobedience led to acts of violence, and soldiers of the colonial army in Amritsar massacred a peaceful crowd of people, Gandhi broke off the campaign: he thought that the population had not understood the meaning of *satyagraha* properly.

In subsequent years he devoted himself completely to constructive programmes: the building up of a new society in India, especially through the encouragement of the native textile industry and crafts (above all spinning and weaving); through programmes for the abolition of the status of untouchables; and through the introduction of educational programmes, above all in country regions. Influenced by Tolstoy and Ruskin, he had already founded communities in South Africa which attempted to live out his principles of non-violence in everyday life and support one another in this process. Although after reading Ruskin's *Unto This Last* he had arrived at the insight that the life of farmers and craftsmen is 'the truly good life', it was only after the Salt March of 1930 and his resignation from the Congress Party at the end of 1934 that he left his ashram in Ahmedabad and went to Wardha in Central India, where in 1936 he founded the Sevagram ashram.

The Salt March from Ahmedabad to Dandi on the Indian Ocean is one of Gandhi's most important *satyagraha* actions. After the rejection of a catalogue of demands made to the British Viceroy, which aimed at great autonomy for India, Gandhi resolved to march with other inhabitants of the ashram to Dandi, there to get salt from the sea water and thus symbolically break the colonial monopoly on salt. In other places, salt depots were stormed by non-violent demonstrations. This action represented the first step in the direction of political independence for India. All that year there were strikes and boycotts throughout the country, although Gandhi had already been arrested and was released only after the one-sided independence ceremonies in 1931. Abolishing the status of untouchability for the outcastes, whom he called 'Harijan', children of God, became the focus of his work the next year: this brought him the bitter opposition of the political leader of the outcastes, Bhimrao Ambedkar. Ambedkar criticized Gandhi for wanting to do away with discrimination against the outcastes but not putting the whole caste system in question. There was a break over the question of separate political representation for the outcastes, which Gandhi rejected in order not to endanger the unity of the Hindus. Ambedkar later led a move into Buddhism.

After years of stagnation in the negotiations over the complete independence of the country, in 1941 Gandhi began the last great campaign with actions of 'individual *satyagraha*' and continued them in 1942 with the 'Quit India' movement. When the situation escalated in 1946 and there were Indian terrorist acts followed by massacres of the Indian civil population, and soon afterwards also unrest between Hindus and Muslims, despite his advanced age Gandhi once again became active in making peace. His fasts and walks on foot through troubled regions could only pacify the situation temporarily and in some places. His commitment to reconciliation between Hindus and Muslims led radical Hindus to plot his murder. On 30 January 1948, six months after India's independence, Gandhi died from the bullets of an assassin in Delhi on the way to a prayer meeting.

Literature

M.K. Gandhi, *Autobiography. The Story of My Experiments with Truth*, Harmondsworth: Penguin Books 1982.

M.K. Gandhi, *Gandhi on Non-Violence. A Selection from the Writings of Mahatma Gandhi*, ed. Thomas Merton, San Francisco: Shambhala Publications 1996.

Judith Brown, *Gandhi, Prisoner of Hope*, New Haven: Yale University Press 1989.

Bhikhu Parekh, *Gandhi*, Oxford: Oxford University Press 1997.

Jayaprakash Narayan

Humanist and analyst

'My world lies in ruins. I fear that I shall never see it put together in the time which still remains to me.' So wrote Jayaprakash Narayan, in India usually known only by his initial J.P, in his *Prison Diary*. Without great sentimentality, the founder of the Socialist Party of India and later activist for non-violent resistance looked back on his political life, which temporarily ended with his arrest by Prime Minister Indira Gandhi in 1975.

Jayaprakash Narayan was born in 1902 in the present state of Bihar in northern India. Already as a schoolboy he felt attracted to the independence movement. Shortly before he left the country for six years to study sociology in the USA, he met Gandhi. As he felt committed to the principle of non-collaboration with the British, he did not accept a grant, and had to earn his living through hard work, among other things on the fruit plantations in California. Here he came into contact with Marxist ideas. This led him again to distance himself from Gandhi's movement; after he returned to India he attached himself to the Indian National Congress and Jawaharlal Nehru. Even during the struggle for independence, he developed from a revolutionary Marxist into a democratic socialist and finally founded the Socialist Party. He was imprisoned several times by the British for involvement in acts of sabotage. In 1953 , disillusioned, he left party politics and played an active part in Vinoba Bhave's land-gift campaign (see p. 80).

In this connection J.P. took on the task of organizing and leading Shanti Sena, a non-violent peace army, founded by Vinoba after an idea of Gandhi's (see p. 80). The efforts of the small Portuguese colony of Goa in South India to gain independence particularly attracted his interest, and there in 1961 he sought by a non-violent invasion to anticipate a solution favoured by the Indian government which was finally in fact carried through by military force. Natayan analysed and criticized the failure of his own movement, and a year later, in the frontier war between India and China, attempted to stop the military actions by a peace march from Delhi to Peking. However, the Chinese authorities stopped the march at the frontier. J.P. had to recognize that peace through non-violence is to be attained less by means of spectacular actions than by long-term constructive work. For this reason, in the following years he mobilized the Shanti Sena to become active in the unrest of north-east India. The peace activists soon won so much trust among the population that rebels of ethnic minorities were prepared to come to the negotiating table in this region. In the river valley of Chambal, in the centre of India, Narayan's initiative and collaboration made an essential contribution towards the peaceful resolution of conflict with armed bands of robbers, a result of social decay. Some of the former robbers even began to get involved in projects to help the socially disadvantaged.

When at the end of the 1960s doubts arose even in the nonviolent movement about the long-term effectiveness of the land-gift and village-gift campaigns, Narayan followed the call of the activists in the especially impoverished Muzzaffarpur district of the federal state of Bihar. There workers of the Sarvodaya movement who appealed to Gandhi were being threatened by Communist rebels, who expressed the growing dissatisfaction of the rural population. Narayan remained in the region in order to counter the violence, but recognized that even in the villages covered by the village-gift movement the impoverished farmers had experienced hardly any change in their situation and now saw revolutionary violence as the ultimate way out of their hopeless situation. Here Narayan revived Vinoba Bhave's view that there was no place in independent India for 'negative' *satyagraha*, i.e. civil disobedience against the state, as opposed to positive *satyagraha*, constructive work for social justice. Vinoba thought that now India was independent it had to be built up. Narayan also opposed Vinoba's idea that class controversy was incompatible with the goal of harmonious relations in the village. He believed that first the neglected needs of the village population had to be taken seriously.

Widespread corruption and high prices led to a general loss of trust in the Indian government and at the beginning of the 1970s sparked off a student movement in Bihar which quickly spread and shook all India. In June 1975, Indira Gandhi felt compelled to declare a state of emergency. As early as the beginning of 1974 the students approached Narayan with a request that he should take over leadership of the movement. After some hesitation he agreed. However, his aim of bringing down the government was not accepted by part of the non-violent movement, although Narayan assured them that it was not his concern to engage in party politics. At a great demonstration which took place on 5 June 1974 in Patna, the capital of Bihar, he gave a programmatic speech which had a tremendous effect. While, even to the amazement of the organizers, more and more people were still streaming into the meeting place, in a statement which later became a slogan he stated that this truly was the beginning of a 'total' revolution, i.e. a revolution embracing all realms of life. He called on the students to go into the villages in order to live there and to organize with the farmers. The declaration of the state of emergency interrupted the dynamic of this movement, which began to change India from below. J.P. did not recover from the damage to his health caused by imprisonment. He just lived to see the end of the state of emergency in 1977 and the formation of a broad alliance of opposition parties, the creation of which can be attributed to his influence. Jayaprakash Narayan did not succeed in linking up again with the movement of 1974/75: he died on 8 October 1979.

Jayaprakash Narayan's political commitment was based on humanity and a nearness to the people, but largely it had no reference to religious or spiritual categories. Nevertheless, his activity in the last three decades of his life was seen as a natural part of the Sarvodaya ('prosperity for all') movement, with its spiritual roots in the thought of Gandhi and Vinoba. He dedicated himself to a sociological description and explanation of social events, but could value Vinoba's achievements in the spiritual sphere. In a conversation about spirituality with the inhabitants of the women's ashram in Paunar in 1971, he said that he had read the Bhagavad-gita as a young man and that this had given him motivation for his commitment. Later he had become an atheist, but in the end he had never felt that a purely material basis for human existence was sufficient. It becomes clear from the notes in his *Prison Diary* that in his last years J.P again grappled with Hindu philosophy and ethics.

People who worked with him report his deeply humanist basic attitude, which had a spiritual influence. As an Indian *karmayogi*, a seeker for truth through practical action, J.P. said: 'If anyone does his work unselfishly, that is already prayer.' He described his vision of social life in the villages of India like this: for a society based on non-violence the feeling that 'we and you are one is a necessary spiritual presupposition'.

Literature

Jayaprakash Narayan, *From Face to Face*, Varanasi: Sarva Seva Sangh Prakashan 1971.

Jayaprakash Narayan, *Prison Diary 1975*, Bombay: Popular Prakashan 1977.

Jayaprakash Narayan, *Towards Total Revolution* (4 vols), Bombay: Popular Prakashan 1978.

BUDDHISM

Aung San Suu Kyi

Loving goodness as the principle of political action

'Saints, it is said, are sinners who continue their efforts. Therefore free people are those oppressed who continue their efforts and in this process make themselves capable of taking responsibility and prizing those disciplines which create a free society. Among the fundamental freedoms for which people strive so that their life is full and unrestricted, freedom from fear towers highest, both as a means and as an end. A people which wants to build up a nation with strong democratic institutions in the face of the caprice of the state must first learn to free its own spirit from apathy and fear.'

Aung San Suu Kyi, who was under house arrest from July 1989 to July 1995, and even after her release continued to be watched by the Burmese military regime, is not afraid of suffering the fate of many murdered, tortured or 'disappeared' democrats in Burma. Fear, she believes, is a habit from which she can free herself through her long years of experience abroad. Fear goes with hatred, and therefore fear can be countered with *metta*, loving goodness. Since in this way trust is created, and one's own insecurity and that of one's fellow-men and women is contested, reconciliation can take place.

It is no coincidence that Aung San Suu Kyi, the daughter of the freedom hero General Aung San, author of the draft of a democratic constitution and co-founder of the Burmese army, found her way into politics. But after her father was murdered when she was two years old, still before the independence of Burma from British colonial rule, initially she went other ways. Born in 1945, she studied politics and economics in Delhi and Oxford, worked from 1969 to 1972 at the United Nations, New York, and in 1972 married Michael Aris, the expert on Tibet, with whom she lived for a while in the Himalayan kingdom of Bhutan. Only in 1988 did Aung San Suu Kyi return to Burma to look after her dying mother, and got involved in the maelstrom of the democratic movement which was just developing.

Just a few weeks after her arrival she experienced how the military regime seemed to counter the growing cries for democracy and then crushed all the people's hopes with a massacre on 8 August 1988, when it opened fire on several thousand non-violent demonstrators. On 26 August 1988 Aung San Suu Kyi publicly declared her entry into politics. At a demonstration attended by half a million people she stated that the basic principles of her political activity were non-violence, the restoration of human rights and the introduction of multi-party democracy. She saw herself treading in the footsteps of her father.

The National League for Democracy (NLD), also founded by Aung San Suu Kyi, of which she soon became president, gained more than 80% of the seats at the elections of 27 May 1990, despite massive hindrance from the military regime. But the generals ignored the convincing result of the vote and did not let Parliament get on with its work. Many members of the NLD were arrested or had to leave the country. At this point Aung San Suu Kyi found herself under house arrest. She did not accept the offer of the military regime to let her go abroad, since she did not want to betray her promise to help the Burmese along the road to democracy. For her, civil disobedience means not yielding to injustice. In the years of her imprisonment she orientated herself on Nelson Mandela and Václav Havel as models, and time and again offered to engage in dialogue with the government in order to overcome the crisis caused by the country's isolation as the result of an international boycott. In 1991 Aung San Suu Kyi received the Nobel Peace Prize.

For this pragmatist, *metta*, loving goodness, is not a sentimental concept with which she overlooks political differences. In Buddhist philosophy *metta* belongs with generosity, patience, meditation, wisdom and reconciliation among the ways to liberation. For Aung San Suu Kyi, whose politics are indissolubly associated with spiritual values, *metta* is an active principle which is meant to create the presuppositions for an open dialogue with political opponents and a pleasant atmosphere of trust. It is not enough to radiate goodness, which is why she emphasizes how important it is to take responsibility oneself and to act.

In general, Aung San Suu Kyi says of herself that she 'believes firmly in action, efforts and endeavour'. She violently challenges those interpretations of the doctrine of *karma* which claim that all suffering is a result of past actions and thus makes it seem immutable: 'I believe that this is an excuse for doing nothing and that it is incompatible with our Buddhist views. If what happens is the result of the past, then there is all the more reason to make every effort today to change the situation.' In her speeches, which since her release from house arrest she gives weekly in front of her house, she keeps pointing out that every person must make an effort towards his or her liberation. She does not want to be singled out as an extraordinary person, but to stimulate others to raise questions and take their fates into their own hands despite the difficult conditions in their homeland.

For the woman who as a young girl wanted to follow her father's example and enter the army, truth is 'a powerful weapon' and non-violence first of all a political tactic. Granted, she thinks that *ahimsa*, non-violence, is a spiritual principle which is based on the five Buddhist commandments (do not kill, do not steal, do not lie, do not engage in sexual misbehaviour, do not take drugs). But she has chosen non-violence in the sense of 'positive action' more as a political tactic, since she thinks that this is the right way to a stable democracy in Burma. She supports the students who after the violent defeat of the democratic movement have engaged in a guerrilla war, but she does not herself want to bring about political change through weapons, because this continues the tradition that power is based on armed force. In actual clashes with armed soldiers, time and again she showed courage, as for example when she once approached a unit of soldiers ready to shoot and sought to engage them in conversation.

Aung San Suu Kyi goes one step further in her description of the causes of injustice and violence. In many speeches and articles she criticizes the policy of the 'new world order' which judges human development exclusively by material criteria and thus destroys the foundations of a civilized society. This is contrary to her ideas: 'In its investigation of the forms of human suffering, Buddhism identifies greed and lust – i.e. passion and devoting oneself to unrestrained desires – as the first of the ten uncleannesses which stand in the way of a quiet, peaceful spiritual state of mind . . . Buddhists understand friendliness, compassion, sympathy, reconciliation as "divine" characteristics which help to relieve distress and disseminate happiness among all beings. The greatest obstacle to these noble feelings is not so much hatred or rage as a bitter state of mind, an existence orientated on narrow-minded selfishness.' She calls for economic, political and social institutions which work in the service of men and women, a culture which attends to human needs, and an authentic participation of people in processes of social and political transformation. Aung San Suu Kyi argues against politicians who reject democracy and human rights as Western influences and as being contrary to the Asian way of development. Poverty, she says, cannot be fought against by material support. Only the sharing of power, and the possibility for people to determine their own freedom and security, will further peace, stability and unity.

Literature

Aung San Suu Kyi, *Freedom from Fear*, Harmondsworth: Penguin
    Books 1995.
Aung San Suu Kyi, *Opening Keynote Address by Aung San Suu Kyi
    read on Video to the NGO Forum on Women*, Beijing 1995.
Aung San Suu Kyi, *The Voice of Hope*, Harmondsworth: Penguin
    Books 1997.

Dalai Lama XIV

Wisdom and compassion

'If we really want to do something for freedom and justice, then
it is best if we do this without rage and hostility. With inner
tranquillity and an honest readiness we can work hard for thirty,
forty years. I believe that some positive results have been achieved
through my clear profession of non-violence, which rests on an
authentic faith that all human beings are sisters and brothers.'

The Fourteenth Dalai Lama, the supreme spiritual and secular
head of the Tibetans, has by now been living for almost forty years
in exile in India. He has become the most popular representative
of Buddhism in the West. The spiritual dreams of many
Europeans and North Americans influenced by Buddhism are
focussed on his country, Tibet. The Dalai Lama utilizes this interest to campaign for support for the rights of the Tibetans
oppressed by China, but he has never had any illusions about the
contradictory nature of the reality of Tibet. He knows that the
social and political system of Tibet before the Chinese invasion
of 1950 and the complete occupation in 1959 was hopelessly
antiquated and corrupt; that the Tibetan economy needed urgent

renewal; and that times had changed irrevocably even for the high-lands of Central Asia. Here he is of the view that the Chinese occu-pation at least had the positive effect that the Tibetans had to grapple with the world and develop new forms of life.

The Dalai Lama, worshipped as Tulka, i.e. as the reincarnation of his predecessor, the Thirteenth Dalai Lama and, in a long chain of existences, of the Bodhisattva Avalokiteshvara, was born in north-eastern Tibet in 1935 the son of a family of peasant farmers. In accordance with the Tibetan-Buddhist tradition, about four years after the death of the Thirteenth Dalai Lama (in 1933) a search party of monks set off from the capital, Lhasa, following signs and prophecies, to find the reincarnation of the Dalai Lama. In the village of Takster they met the two-year-old Lhamo Thöndup, who confidently picked out of a series of utensils which the search party had brought with them those of the dead Dalai Lama. The child settled in a neighbouring monastery, but because of political obstacles did not make the three-month journey to Lhasa until the summer of 1939. The next year he was instituted as supreme spiritual head of the Tibetan Buddhists and a little later was ordained novice. He was given the monastic name Tenzin Gyatso. Initially the business of rule remained in the hands of regents, who at the same time were the tutors of the growing Dalai Lama. He devoted himself to his education, especially to the study of Buddhist scriptures, philosophy and the art of debating. The child grew up in solitude in the Potala palace, the seat of govern-ment which had been rebuilt in the seventeenth century by the Fifth Dalai Lama. There he became interested in technology and science and already as a young man got involved in the intrigues in the Tibetan government.

In November 1950, when Chinese troops had already occupied the western provinces of Tibet and were about to march on Lhasa, it was decided to institute the Dalai Lama prematurely as supreme political head of Tibet. Evidently this was meant to contribute to the stabilization of the country. Nevertheless the People's

Republic of China carried through the establishment of a parallel Chinese administration in Tibet, and in the course of the years sent more and more troops to Lhasa. In the provinces the population began to rebel against the Chinese, who ruled with brutal oppression, and to offer armed resistance – not least with the half-hearted support of the CIA. The Dalai Lama, by then fifteen, continued his study, which he completed only in 1959, fruitlessly made contact with the United Nations, and in 1954 travelled to China, there to negotiate with Mao in person over the independence of Tibet. This attempt by the still inexperienced young politician was as vain as conversations with Jawaharlal Nehru and other Indian politicians on a journey to Sikkim and India in 1956/57. Still, at that time modern Tibet for the first time broke its self-chosen policy of isolation and entered the arena of international diplomacy.

Famines and the repression of the Chinese People's Army, which were becoming intolerable, led in March 1959 to a Tibetan revolt in Lhasa, the repression of which, according to Chinese sources, claimed more than 80,000 human lives. The Dalai Lama, increasingly under pressure to justify his policy of entente with China, escaped to India, in disguise and under the protection of rebels. There he devoted himself to the organization and development of the Tibetan refugee community and the establishment of an exile regime in Dharamsala in northern India. Indefatigably, on journeys all over the world he still campaigns for a recognition of the independent state of Tibet – increasingly vainly, given the openness of China to the West. Granted, in 1989 he received the Nobel Peace Prize and is respected as a spiritual and moral authority, but time is running out for him in Tibet: the Chinese policy of settlement and waves of refugees have already made the Tibetans a minority in their own land. Therefore today the Dalai Lama no longer calls for the complete political independence of Tibet, but only for sufficient guarantees that Tibetan values and culture will be preserved.

Today, as in the 1950s, the Dalai Lama finds himself exposed to criticism when he argues against the armed battle for liberation. In the face of the overwhelming Chinese supremacy, with Chinese economic and military superiority ranged against the six million people of Tibet, he saw (and still sees) no sense in a guerrilla war which would shed much blood. Nor, realistically, did he want to rely on unofficial support from the USA, which was offered him through the CIA. But to these pragmatic considerations are added matters of principle: 'In practice we can achieve something by violence, but only at the expense of the prosperity of someone else. In this way we perhaps solve one problem, but at the same time create another. The best way of solving problems is by human understanding, mutual respect. Perhaps full satisfaction will not be achieved, but at least future dangers will be avoided. Non-violence is a more certain way.'

Nevertheless, non-violent actions which in their constructive nature correspond most closely to human nature are not always just gentle. In accordance with Buddhist thought, in which right intentions play a major role, the Dalai Lama writes: 'It is hard to decide by outward appearances whether an action is violent or non-violent. This ultimately depends on the motivation of the action. If the motivation is negative, the action is in a deeper sense very violent, even if outwardly it is very binding and friendly. On the other hand, harsh measures and words which come from an honest positive motivation are fundamentally non-violent. In other words, violence is a destructive power. Non-violence is constructive.'

For a man who sees religion and politics as being closely connected, such non-violent action is religious action. His concern is that people today should assume a universal sense of responsibility for the situation of the planet as a whole and for one another. The basis for this is altruism and compassion and the combating of inner enemies like pride, anger or jealousy – this is what he calls 'real religious practice'. He believes that only in this way, and not through pressure to accept responsibility, can there be a solution to the social, political and ecological problems – a clear departure from the purely materialistic models which he still admired among Mao's Communists during his first visit to China and from which he had also hoped impulses would come for the development of Tibet.

The Dalai Lama endeavours to orientate his life on the *bodhisattva* ideal: 'According to the Buddhist view a *bodhisattva* is someone on the way to Buddhahood who devotes his whole life to the task of liberating all other beings from suffering . . . The *bodhisattva* ideal is therefore the effort to practise infinite compassion in infinite wisdom.' He believes that true compassion can bring about a positive move towards peace and draws hope for a growth of world peace from the observation that even powerful states are beginning to see the need to respect the truth and to make room for both human rights and democratic freedoms.

Literature

Dalai Lama XIV, *Autobiography. Freedom in Exile*, London and New York: Abacus Books 1995.

Dalai Lama XIV, *The Way to Freedom*, San Francisco: HarperCollins 1995.

Dalai Lama XIV, *The Joy of Living and Dying in Peace*, San Francisco: HarperCollins 1995.

Maha Ghosananda

Peace step by step

'We must summon up the courage to leave our own temples and go into the temples of human experience, temples which are full of suffering. If we listen to the Buddha, to Christ or to Gandhi, there is nothing else for us to do. Then the refugee camps, the prisons, the ghettos and the battlefields will be our temples.'

In 1978 the monk Maha Ghosananda left the temple in Thailand where he had meditated for thirteen years to return to his homeland of Cambodia. In the middle of the 1960s that South-East Asian land had been drawn into the Vietnam war; since 1969 it had had to suffer US bombing raids, and since 1975 the murderous regime of the Khmer Rouge. More than 2 million people, including almost all the intellectuals and the bulk of the Buddhist clergy, fell victim to the mad attempt to create a new society.

Maha Ghosananda entered Cambodia shortly before the Khmer Rouge were driven into the forests by an invasion from Vietnam. 'Do not fight with suffering. Find your own way' – he followed this principle of Buddhist non-violence. First of all he made contact with refugees in Cambodia and then also with Cambodian communities scattered all over the world. In the subsequent years of the civil war the monk sought conversation with all the parties in the conflict. The aim of his efforts was and still is a lasting peace in predominantly Buddhist Cambodia. In 1991 the warring parties signed a peace treaty which in 1993 led to elections under UN supervision. But only a limited normality has replaced the civil war; time and again fighting is reported from distant parts of the land and everywhere buried landmines will go on killing people for decades.

Maha Ghosananda was born in 1929, the son of peasants in the Mekong Delta. Growing up in a community of Buddhist monks was typical of the societies of South and South-East Asia which are adherents of Theravada Buddhism – the oldest school: as an eight-year-old temple boy in the village temple he was responsible for menial tasks and thus had the opportunity to get to know temple life more closely. At the age of fourteen he was ordained novice. Later the young monk studied in various universities in Cambodia and in India, the land from which Buddhist teaching origi-nated. There he came into contact with the founder of the Japanese Nipponzan-Myohoji sect, the monk Nichidatsu Fujii. The Nipponzan monks did outstanding peace work and had an active understanding of non-violence.

After some years in Cambodia, which he had spent near the supreme head of the Cambodian monastic community, in 1965 Maha Ghosananda went to the south of Thailand. A movement had come into being there in the forest temples which combined a strict practice of meditation with a social conscience. Some years later he learned there of the beginning of war in his homeland: 'They told us that we were not to allow the war in Cambodia to influence our spirit. We should not allow it to disturb our concen-tration. Nevertheless, every day we wept for Cambodia.'

Maha Ghosananda sees control of one's own spirit as the funda-mental principle of Buddhist teaching which creates peace: 'If we control the spirit, we are free from all suffering. No other teaching is needed.' Here he finds himself firmly in the meditative tradition of Buddhist renewal in the twentieth century, which puts mind control as a principle for behaviour in the foreground. 'Right mind control' is the seventh element of the Noble Eightfold Path for overcoming suffering as taught by the Buddha. A whole series of techniques has been developed for this, for example concentra-tion on the breath. Thai monks in the past century have investi-gated the Noble Eightfold Path (right views, right attitude of mind, right speech, right conduct, right way of life, right effort, right mind control, right meditation) to see what possibilities it offers for social change.

So Maha Ghosananda says: 'Mind control and clear understanding form the heart of Buddhist meditation. Peace is achieved when we control our minds at every step.' His personal commitment puts him above any suspicion that he understands this only as an individual way to salvation.

According to Ghosananda, peace begins with the individual: to love oneself, to protect oneself, to care for oneself, to see that one is happy. Loving goodness as the practice of Buddhist non-violence is built on this – the effort not to do any harm and to be devoted to the well-being of all men and women. The Sanskrit word *ahimsa* is used for this in the Buddhist tradition.

Here non-violence is in no way synonymous with political naivety. Time and again Ghosananda points out that compassion and wisdom belong together. He interprets the principle of the middle way, which is often quoted in Buddhism, as a balance between wisdom and compassion. He tells the following story. A peasant finds a dying poisonous snake, which he puts in his bed to cure it. But as soon as it is healthy it bites the peasant, who dies from the venom. 'Compassion without wisdom can cause great suffering.'

At the political level, approach to the Khmer Rouge as those responsible for the genocide does not mean failing to condemn their actions. Ghosananda is convinced that compassion and wisdom correspond to humanitarian needs and political reality. 'It means to have compassion without making concessions, and to make peace without sweeping things under the carpet.' He is working for a resolution of conflicts from which all parties emerge as victors. However, he has his own way of doing this. First of all it meant going into the refugee camps, including those controlled by the Khmer Rouge, to support reconciliation there and rebuild the Cambodian monastic orders. In 1988 Maha Ghosananda was nominated supreme head of the Cambodian Buddhists.

Since 1992, in April and May he has led annual peace marches (*dhamma yietra* – pilgrimage of justice, the right way of life) through Cambodia; in particular they are aimed at building up trust in the peace process in insecure regions. When the assembled activists came under fire at the beginning of a peace march and survived grenade attacks only by luck, he did not call a halt to the proceedings: this was the very reason for continuing to march. His motto that peace comes into being 'step by step' has become proverbial in Cambodia. It is not an empty formula, for 'to create peace we must first remove the landmines in our hearts which prevent us from making peace: hatred, greed and deception.' This is the foundation of his commitment to the international campaign against landmines and the efforts to remove them from Cambodia, which has vast stretches of mined land.

Literature

Maha Ghosananda, *Step to Step: Meditations on Wisdom and Compassion*, Berkeley: Parallax Press 1993.
Kim Teng Nhem, 'Working Slowly towards Peace in Cambodia', in Ed Garcia (ed.), *Pilgrim Voices: Citizens as Peacemakers*, Manila: Ateno de Manila University Press 1994.

Stella Tamang

Learning with head, heart and hand

'For me, non-violence is both active and passive. If we practise it in order to encounter active violence with it, then it is active. In the real sense non-violence is so peaceful, clear and cool.' So says the Nepalese Buddhist Stella Tamang. The educationalist and activist radiates this repose and self-certainty and combines both in her everyday life with much pragmatism and organizational skill. She founded her first school when she was only a twenty-two-year-old student; at first the school was not recognized by the education ministry because the equipment was very simple – she had had to finance the institution privately. Undeterred, she continued her work, and when only six months later more than fifty children were being taught, official recognition of the school experiment also followed.

Stella Tamang, who was born in 1954, grew up in Burma and first went to Nepal, her parents' homeland, at the age of fifteen. Her father was a Lama, a priest of the Tibetan Kagyukpa sect. Through him she got an insight into the thought of Mahayana Buddhism, the so-called 'great vehicle' of Buddhist teaching, which is predominant in Central and East Asia. However, the environment of her youth in Burma is stamped by Theravada Buddhism, the 'school of the elders', which is determinative in Sri Lanka and South-East Asia. This varied experience makes it easy for her even today to get involved in collaboration which extends beyond particular regions; she does this as a member of the Executive Committee of the International Network of Engaged Buddhists, founded in 1989 by the Thai social critic Sulak Sivaraksa.

Stella Tamang completed her schooling in difficult economic conditions and wanted to study medicine. Nothing came of this dream for financial reasons, so she accepted a post as an auxiliary teacher, which allowed her to study English literature, economics and education in the morning and evening lessons. At this time she began to reflect on the Nepalese educational system. She recognized that traditional schooling would not solve the problems faced by the ordinary population of Nepal. The school system was caught up in a model of development which took no notice of the knowledge present locally. 'It is based on wisdom, energy and power from outside – always a dependent model which neglects the inner sources of human energy and power. The result of such misdirected models of development is that spiritual, emotional, social damage is done to people. This is damage which is not always easily seen or recognized.'

She began to reflect on a model of development which takes up local traditions and treats people's social values seriously. Her own situation as a member of the Buddhist Tamang tribe, which was in a minority over against the Hindus who ran the state, made it particularly clear to her that development benefits only a particular group of the population. Stella's marriage to Parshuram Tamang, the president of the Tamang association and general secretary of the umbrella organization for twenty-four associations of Nepalese groups, brought her closer to this problem. The Tamang are among the largest ethnic groups in Nepal, but at the same time they are most affected by poverty and illiteracy. Especially Buddhist women, whose religion or tribal traditions traditionally accorded women more rights than Hindus, hoped that the democratization of Nepal in the 1980s and beginning of the 1990s would bring a recognition of their position. In particular they were allowed divorce and possessions, and they could inherit land. But the new constitution prescribed Hinduism as the state religion and thus made their status worse. Together with members of other religious communities, the Buddhists therefore supported a secular state in Nepal which respected the religious and social identity of the tribal population.

In Stella Tamang's own school, named 'Bhrikuti' after a seventeenth-century princess, today about 900 children are taught, of all ages. The founder's aim is 'a change of one's person, society and the world by strengthening human values'. Therefore great attention is paid to spirituality and the reciprocal relations between different groups and cultures in the everyday life of the school. The children are to discover, experience and understand the truth in many ways, with head, heart and hand. Stella Tamang takes seriously the Buddhist principle that wisdom is needed to know the truth. The tradition of the sayings of Buddha holds that nothing is to be believed without being tested.

Here Stella Tamang follows the Buddhist tradition, which aims at the individual responsibility of people for their own further development. However, it combines this responsibility with the social responsibility formulated particularly during the twentieth century in the Buddhist societies of South-East Asia and with an effort to form and preserve communities. The children for whom it is responsible do not learn just in the school. Nature and their social environment offer further fields of learning. Moreover the parents are involved in the teaching. To make this possible, the Bhrikuti school is concerned to make access possible for poorer children – by the pattern of education and by reducing costs.

But not all parts of society can be reached in this way. Many children must contribute to the support of their family from as early an age as five and cannot afford the time for school education. In the tribal population there is mistrust of an educational system which uses the language of the dominant culture. Therefore Stella Tamang and a growing group of colleagues have developed the concept of 'alternative centres of education' which are particularly focussed on working girls, as these are among the weakest members of society.

In these centres, skills in traditional crafts and in reading and writing are communicated. The use of local experiences and materials can meet the need to earn money where people live. The carpet industry, the branch of Nepalese industry with the greatest proportion of child labour, is concentrated in the cities because it uses imported wool. In the past that led to girls being hired or sold to the cities. International pressure to end child labour led to this practice being continued only in secret. When girls are sacked they are often compelled to earn their living by prostitution – Nepalese society is heavily involved in the human trade in the conurbations of the Indian subcontinent.

To counter this, in the 'alternative centres of education' Stella

Tamang concentrates each year on one ethnic group in whose language she arranges the teaching, and on participants from one region. The encouragement to produce locally can help people to regain their dignity by learning once again to assess the value of their own traditions. For Stella Tamang, this knowledge is fundamental to her political work: at the Asian level through her presidency of the 'Programme for Indigenous Knowledge', and internationally by collaboration with the aid to children given by UNICEF. She sees her involvement as being connected with an alternative model of development for the whole country: 'Every human being has the right to live in dignity and to be proud of his or her culture. The women and children of the tribal peoples are the most severely oppressed and neglected members of Nepalese society. But Nepal could not develop without their labour force. We have fought for our own survival and now we are helping others who are fighting.'

Thich Nhat Hanh

Teacher of mind control

On 4 April 1968 the Vietnamese Zen monk Thich Nhat Hanh took part in the eucharist with the US Franciscan Daniel Berrigan. Their friendship was a sign of the efforts for peace being made at a time when North American troops had intervened in the Vietnam war. Both men were later criticized by members of their faith communities for taking part in the ceremony. That same evening they heard a lecture by Hans Küng and learned that the Civil Rights champion Martin Luther King had been murdered. King had proposed Thich Nhat Hanh for the Nobel Peace Prize two years previously.

The Zen monk speaks of the 'living Buddha' and the 'living Christ', and statues of both stand on his household altar, because he regards them as his spiritual forebears. But Thich Nhat Hanh concedes that his way to grappling openly with Christianity was a long one. First of all he experienced the Christian mission in the French colonial period and the prohibition of Buddhist festivals by the Catholic dictator of South Vietnam, Ngo Dinh Diem. But later encounters with Martin Luther King, whom he regarded as a saint, Daniel Berrigan, and the activists of the Fellowship of Reconciliation, would decisively alter his attitude.

Thich Nhat Hanh was born in 1926 with the civil name Nguyen Xuan Bao, and entered a Zen monastery at the age of sixteen. At the beginning of the 1960s he studied comparative religion in the USA, but during the war, in 1964, he returned to Vietnam. In Saigon he founded the 'School of Youth for Social Service', through which he wanted to put Buddhist thought into concrete practice in society. In courses lasting up to six months, young men and women were prepared for social tasks in the villages and slums; they were to provide aid particularly in the increasingly deteriorating situation in the rural areas of Vietnam. Thich Nhat Hanh was convinced that a democratic development of his country would be possible only on the basis of social and economic development. However, the social workers trained in this school were increasingly used to mitigate the effects of war, and in 1975, after the agreement between North and South Vietnam, their activity was completely prohibited. Thich Nhat Hanh, who in 1966 had been invited by the International Fellowship of Reconciliation to give a lecture tour in the USA, had to remain in exile. As early as 1965 the South Vietnamese government had banned his book of peace poems. The same year he founded the Buddhist order of Interbeing.

Thich Nhat Hanh gave an impressive description of the suffering of Vietnamese people in the war and thus made the term 'engaged Buddhism' known at an international level. The Trappist Thomas

Merton called Thich Nhat Hanh his brother and wrote: 'He has come to us, like others before him, to bear witness to the spirit of Zen. More clearly than others, he has shown us that Zen is not an esoteric and world-denying cult of inner illumination, but has an unusual and unique sense of responsibility in our modern world.'

For Thich Nhat Hanh, engaged Buddhism is first his own practice of mind control in daily life. From this he derives the strength for work on social and political problems. 'I have been active in peace work for more than thirty years. I have fought against poverty, ignorance and disease and have been to sea to help with the rescue of boat people. I have evacuated the wounded from the battlefields, returned refugees to their homeland, helped hungry children and orphans, spoken out against the war, written and disseminated peace literature, taught peace workers and social workers and rebuilt bombed villages. Only by the practice of meditation – inward repose and deep contemplation – could I protect and nourish the sources of my spiritual energy and continue this work.'

Today Thich Nhat Hanh lives in the south-west of France in a monastery called Plum Village, a community of Vietnamese, Europeans and North Americans, and teaches meditation and mind control. 'Real peace must be based on insight and understanding. For this we must practise deep reflection – regard in depth every action and every thought in our daily life. With mind control, the practice of peace, we can begin to transform the wars in ourselves. There are techniques for this. Conscious breathing is one.'

When we practice mind control, we find the repose to live in the present moment; we neither investigate the past nor plan the future. In this way it becomes possible 'really to be there to touch on life'. Thich Nhat Hanh describes how this affects the capacity to listen, the capacity to recognize happiness, rage, sorrow and deep hurts, and to deal with them consciously. For him as a Buddhist the energy which arises out of compassion – not that which emerges out of anger – is the only sure energy which can change society positively. Therefore he advises the practice of mind control in all everyday actions, by observation of the breath or in meditations during walks. 'If we nurture mind control every day and water the seed of peace in us and in the people around us, we have a chance to prevent the next war and to blunt the next crisis.'

Mind control helps us to develop compassion for others. It is hardest to develop compassion for opponents or for people who have inflicted great suffering on others. Therefore Thich Nhat Hanh has emphasized the Buddhist principle of non-separation, deep participation and responsibility even for the actions of others which are to be repudiated. When he went to Thailand in 1975 to help in the rescue of the so-called Boat People, he heard of a little girl who had been raped by pirates and who had thrown herself into the sea. Thich Nhat Hanh reports the helpless rage and sorrow which he felt when he got the news. Here the principle of non-separation means being able to identify both with the victim and with the perpetrator. He wrote about this in his poem 'Call me by my true name':

> I am the twelve-year-old girl
> on a little refugee boat
> who throws herself into the sea
> after she has been raped by a pirate,
> and I am also the pirate,
> my heart is not yet ready to see and to love . . .
> Please call me by my true name
> so that I can hear all my cries and my laughter
> at the same time,
> so that I can see
> that my joy and my sorrow are one . . .

With this attitude, Thich Nhat Hanh was always particularly tested when he gave courses for Vietnam veterans, the US soldiers who had fought in his homeland. One of them, Claude Thomas, reports how Thich Nhat Hanh spoke to them: 'You veterans are the light above the candle. You burn hot. You have the capacity, as a result of your experience of the world, to help to transform it, to change violence, to change hatred, to change despair. You must speak.'

Literature

Thich Nhat Hanh, *The Lotus in the Sea of Fire*, London: SCM Press 1967.

Thich Nhat Hanh, *Love in Action. Writings on Nonviolent Social Change*, Berkeley: Parallax Press 1993.

Thich Nhat Hanh, *The Miracle of Being Awake*, Dublin: Movement Publications nd.

Fred Eppsteiner (ed.), *The Path of Compassion. Writings on Socially Engaged Buddhism*, Berkeley: Parallax Press 1988.

Claude Thomas, 'Finding Peace After', *Shambhala Sun*, November 1993, 18–23, 62.

II. An A-Z of Non-Violence

Auschwitz and Holocaust

'What lesson can be learned from "Auschwitz"?', asked Thomas Merton, the model for a whole generation of non-violent activists, and here the name of this greatest concentration camp is a symbol for the whole extermination machinery of the National Socialists. What shook him when he reflected on the organized murder in Auschwitz and the trials of the perpetrators, especially Eichmann, was the fact that it all seemed so normal: the perpetrators were psychologically healthy, not tormented by any guilt feelings and practised all the recognized modern virtues. The involvement of quite ordinary people who did not oppose what was going on; who occasionally found the involvement in murder unpleasant yet continued with it; who drew benefit from it and sometimes perhaps even enjoyed exceeding the limits – according to Merton, all this makes the repetition of Auschwitz elsewhere at another time quite conceivable. He concluded that it was necessary to take fundamental truths seriously and act in accordance with them without being assimilated: 'Perhaps in a society like ours the worst abnormality is to be totally free from fear, totally "healthy".'

It is impossible here to engage in an adequate and appropriate discussion of the Holocaust and Auschwitz in connection with non-violent action. Nevertheless we should not pass the theme by, since this could all too easily be misunderstood as an attempt to keep silent about a difficult problem. For how and in what conditions non-violent action is conceivable after German Fascism and after Auschwitz is one of the most serious challenges to the non-violent movements and is a preoccupation not least of Jewish reflection on non-violence. However, we can touch on only the main lines of the course of the discussion here. At the centre is the question, 'Could National Socialism have been resisted with non-violent methods?'

For Jews, pacifist and non-violent action is inconceivable today without reference to Auschwitz. Jewish doubts about non-violence are nurtured by reflection on whether resolute resistance by the Jews in Germany and Europe could possibly have prevented the murder of the five to six million Jews. This resembles the way in which victims accuse themselves about the crimes that have been committed against them. But the repudiation of non-violence and the general assent to military attempts at resolving conflict find supporting arguments here. 'We cannot make free decisions unless we rid ourselves of the feeling that we acted wrongly last time,' writes the Jewish historian Evelyn Wilcock, a specialist on Jewish pacifism in this century. The need to make sure by one's own measures that the Holocaust is not repeated make it difficult for non-violent approaches to get a foothold in the Jewish world after Auschwitz.

So Evelyn Wilcock adds, 'If we Jews allow the Holocaust to dictate to us a withdrawal from peace movements, our absence could contain a message about what Judaism means.' She argues that Jewish non-violence has to be strengthened, precisely because it opposes identification with the murderers. The history of the Holocaust shows that the non-violent resistance of minorities saved Jews from extermination. Therefore it is necessary and possible for Jews themselves also to assert their tradition of non-violence.

'If I were a Jew who was born in Germany, I . . . would claim Germany as my home in the same way as the most non-Jewish German and I would challenge him to shoot me or to throw me in prison; I would refuse to be driven out or to submit to discriminatory treatment.'

With this remark published after the organized attacks on Jewish businesses and synagogues on 9 and 10 November 1938, Mahatma Gandhi provoked a series of indignant reactions in the

Jewish world. Gandhi, who had hesitated to make his statement, compared the civil disobedience of the Indians in South Africa which he had organized with the attitude of the Jews in Germany and proposed that the Jews should oppose the persecution with non-violent means in a voluntary readiness to suffer. Gandhi fully recognized the readiness of the Hitler regime for organized violence, and wrote in a later publication that Jews who offered non-violent opposition had little chance of surviving the Nazi persecution. The liberal Jewish thinker Martin Buber, who a few months previously had settled in Israel, reacted to Gandhi's article, as did the US American rabbi and pacifist Judah L. Magnes, whose letter Gandhi probably never received; so also did the journalist Hayim Greenberg and the Indian Jew A.E. Shohet, who also engaged in direct exchanges with Gandhi. They all made it clear that the situation of the European Jews was fundamentally different from that of the Indians in South Africa and that the comparison was inadmissible. Buber did not believe that *satyagraha*, Gandhi's 'power of love', could be used if the perpetrators did not have a minimum of moral awareness: 'Testimony with no witnesses, ineffective, unobserved, lost martyrdom is the fate of countless Jews in Germany . . . Such martyrdom is done, but who can require it?' Magnes sees no real possibility of practical success for a *satyagraha* of the Jews in Germany as sketched by Gandhi.

However, Gandhi's reflections took into account the costs and the possible success of violent resistance or a war, so that in 1940 he wrote: 'The cause of freedom becomes a farce if the price that has to be paid for freedom consists in exterminating to the utmost degree those who are to enjoy such freedom.' In 1938 resistance which promised success could still perhaps have been offered, against Hitler's preparations for genocide and war – but this resistance would have had to be offered by non-Jewish Germans who were not being persecuted. With the beginning of the war and the abandonment of moral norms that went with it, the apparatus of extermination which to that point had been developed without great protest could be taken further and used for a crime the extent of which still horrifies us and makes us doubt whether there were any non-violent ways out of it. However, the peace scholar Theodor Ebert believes that even a totalitarian regime without a war to conceal its racist policy of extermination could not have justified and maintained such a policy. Ebert connects Gandhi's fear that National Socialism could be conquered by military force only through a 'counter-Hitlerism which overtrumped him' with the nuclear threat to humankind. He argues that nuclear weapons have been legitimized because after 1945 military liberation seemed to be the only conceivable strategic means against totalitarian regimes.

That non-violent action could be successful against Nazi policy in certain conditions is shown by the way in which Danish Jews were helped to escape. Danish politicians had first been able to use political means to prevent the transportation of the Jews after the German occupation. But when Germany wanted to enforce the imprisonment of the Jews, the Danish resistance organized their flight and arranged transport to Sweden. In this way it proved possible to save almost the whole of the Jewish population of Denmark. Alongside the steadfastness of the Danish government, the great public solidarity and the support for the Jews mobilized above all by the Protestant churches contributed to the success of the rescue action. A similar example is the non-violent resistance of the village of Chambon-sur-Ligon in the Cévennes, whose inhabitants under the leadership of the Protestant pastors André Trocmé and Edouard Theis saved the lives of more than twenty-five thousand Jews between 1942 and 1945.

The non-violent protests of the women in Berlin's Rosenstrasse in February and March 1943 are an impressive example of how non-violent resistance against the genocide was possible even in Germany. At the end of February 1943 the Gestapo in Berlin arrested hundreds of German Jews who had been married to 'Aryan' Germans or were the children of so-called 'mixed marriages'. In a short while the non-Jewish wives gathered in Rosenstrasse, where they supposed their imprisoned husbands to be, very near to Gestapo headquarters. When the demonstrators would not break up despite the threats of the police and SS, the arrested men were released and the persecution of those involved in so-called 'mixed marriages' in Germany largely stopped. The success was also affected by the fact that at that time the Nazi regime could not allow any domestic unrest.

The protest of the women in Rosenstrasse remained unnoticed for a long time in the post-war years, and only came to public attention as a result of an article in *Der Spiegel*. The South African Wolfram Kistner, who is of German descent, conjectures that one probable reason why events like this were not discussed in Germany for a long time was that they suggest that more resistance could have been offered to National Socialism with non-violent means than has always been assumed. However, this view was inappropriate in Germany, which after 1945 was caught up in the deterrent strategies of the Cold War.

After the end of the Cold War, non-violent activists saw it as their task to take the difficult way to reconciliation after Auschwitz. The German organization Sühnezeichen/Friedensdienste (Signs of Atonement in the Service of Peace), which has close relations with the Protestant churches, works with young people in voluntary work to assimilate the past and at the same time ensure that the genocide is not forgotten.[1] Quite a different initiative went beyond assimilation of the past. In 1994/95 there was a peace march lasting eight months, from Auschwitz to Hiroshima, organized by the Japanese Buddhist order Nipponzan-Myohoji, which is dedicated to peace worldwide: this connected the Holocaust with war and injustice today. The programme of the demonstration, which was very sensitively prepared, contained

1. The organization understands its commitment as a work of atonement. Whether after Auschwitz there can be atonement and reconciliation in the real sense is utterly rejected by the Jewish side.

not only occasions for interfaith prayer for the activists who had travelled from all over the world, but also the opportunity to hear reports from descendants of Holocaust survivors and Nazi soldiers and to exchange views about their own experiences with and work against crimes against humanity – for example in Bosnia and Rwanda. Here the beginnings of an attempt were made at what peace researchers like Gene Sharp or Theodor Ebert have been calling for for years: indicating the possibilities of non-violent action against a totalitarian regime and mass annihilation by grappling critically with the terrors of the past.

Civil disobedience and non-violent resistance

Non-violent action is implementation of the recognition that people do not always do what is expected of them – sometimes they offend against laws. If the action is taken in the awareness of defending particular values – life, justice – against injustice, and moreover if this is done with a discipline which excludes violence as a means in the struggle, then we have civil disobedience. The people who practise it do not submit to the order which is maintained with police, the army, threats of punishment or other sanctions, but let the apparatus of power run free. However, civil disobedience becomes most radically visible where the regulations are violated openly, where the people practising it show a readiness to run the risk of suffering and disadvantage because of it and are willing to be called to account. Civil disobedience seeks to change violence and injustice, but not to destroy the opponents. In breaking rules or taking them to an absurd length, people define the rules of the game, and become partners in the discussion of the truth.

The US theologian Walter Wink describes this mechanism with

parables from the New Testament. 'If someone strikes you on your right cheek, offer him the other' (Matthew 5.39). Wink thinks that with these statements Jesus, who refused to repay like with like, made it clear how people should behave in the face of an insult. For the chastisement of inferiors in a society in which the use of the left hand was taboo was inflicted as a blow with the back of the right hand; that is the only way in which someone standing in front of you can be struck on the right cheek. So the situation to which Jesus was referring was punishment and insult inflicted on a subordinate by a condescending blow with the back of the hand. Jesus excluded two of the conceivable responses, the passive endurance of injustice and violent reaction with the same means, and commended the third way – the victim is to offer the left cheek and thus compel the person he is facing to hit him with the flat of the hand or the fist. That would inevitably cause difficulties to a superior in the social hierarchy, as it would amount to a recognition of the other as an equal.

'And if anyone compels you to go one mile, go two with him' (Matthew 5.41) refers to a Roman law according to which a soldier was allowed to force civilians from the subject population to carry his pack up to a mile. No more was allowed. After that the soldier had to find someone else. The law, which was probably meant to prevent unrest in the provinces of the Roman empire being provoked frivolously, would inevitably involve a soldier in conflict if someone refused to give up the pack again after a mile. All at once the subject had regained the initiative and inwardly had freed himself from the oppressive power of violence. The joke of it would be that the oppressor was put in a situation in which he had to make decisions for which he was not prepared, to choose to ask for his pack back or to run the risk of being punished for a breach of the law.

Walter Wink put these well-known biblical passages in their historical context to show the white Christians of South Africa how civil disobedience upsets an excessively powerful system. The

South African pastor Christiaan Frederick Beyers Naudé showed how resistance can require extreme stamina and calls for a high degree of spirituality. When he resigned his posts in the white Dutch Reformed Church in 1964 after working in it for twenty-three years because he did not see how racial segregation in the church could be compatible with God's command, he knew that he would probably spend years in solitude. Things got even worse: in 1977 he was banned from making any public appearance for seven years because of his continued actions against apartheid. The ban, which could not rob Beyers Naudé of his deep faith in the Christian task of justice, his love of others, his inner freedom and the spirit of independence, unmasked the injustice of the system, which could not tolerate criticism from the ranks of the whites either. Beyers Naudé regarded these years as the most difficult years of his life, but also the most fruitful. Soon after the ban was lifted he was nominated General Secretary of the South African Council of Churches.

Thomas Merton had in mind the unity of means and ends in non-violent action when he said provocatively that Christian non-violence is not a means of 'taking part in the battles in the world without having to be smeared with blood'. Merton shows with great clarity what non-violence means: 'Anyone who offers non-violent resistance must in reality dissociate himself from his own immediate interests and those of any particular group. He must devote himself to the defence of truth and justice and above all the defence of men and women. He does not want simply to get the upper hand or demonstrate that he is right and his opponents wrong, or to move them to fall in line so that they do what is required of them.' For Merton, non-violent resistance is an attempt to establish the kingdom of God and a concern that all can enter the kingdom. In addition to personal honesty and good will it is necessary for one's actions to be rooted in religion so that life becomes an ongoing transformation and conversion. In his view, 'Blessed are the meek' (Matthew 5.5) does not refer to a placid temperament or passivity but to Christian non-violent action 'trusting in the power of the Lord of truth', action which is not predominantly done in human strength.

In the face of increasing restrictions for asylum seekers, a particular form of civil disobedience has spread in Germany, namely church asylum. A whole series of Catholic and Protestant communities have already granted people asylum in their churches – because there is well-founded doubt about the correctness of a decision by the authorities, in order to gain time for threatened refugees to get permits, in order to be able to end legal proceedings possibly pending against those who have been refused asylum, in order to draw attention to the human rights of the refugees, or as a protest against the erosion of basic rights.

In Islam, submission to the will of an indivisible God is the basis of reflection on civil disobedience and non-collaboration with injustice. Therefore there is even a need for resistance. A Muslim may not obey unjust laws. If he is compelled to do so and there is no longer any possibility of non-violent action, all that is left to him is the solution already practised by the Prophet Muhammad, namely to depart from (Hijra) the society in which he lives and build up a new one under more favourable conditions. After the analysis of a protest action against continued violations of civil rights in Pattani in southern Thailand, Chaiwat Satha-Anand, a Thai Muslim scholar, comes to the conclusion that the religious practice of Muslims prepares them for 'the possibility of disobedience, discipline, interest in social affairs and concrete action, patience and the readiness to fight for a cause, and the idea of unity – all this is decisive for successful non-violent action.' Khalid Kishtainy sees civil disobedience as a 'civil *jihad*', as a fight to establish the divine law.

Mahatma Gandhi coined the term *satyagraha* (persisting in, holding firm to, the truth) and presupposed as essential qualities for the *satyagrahi*, those engaged in civil disobedience, self-discipline, self-control, self-purification and readiness for sacrifice:

'*Satyagraha* is also called power of the soul because a particular knowledge of the inner soul is necessary if a *satyagrahi* is not to believe that death does not mean the end of a fight, but its climax.' Gandhi put great demands on people who committed themselves to *satyagraha*. Their action had to be focussed, they had to prepare themselves well, adopt a clear moral attitude and be aware of their motivation. Gandhi's aim was to convert opponents in the conflict, to bring about a change of heart. To exert exclusively political pressure is not enough for him: the meaning must be indirect and communicated in an indirect way. The demands are so high that Gandhi once broke off an action of civil disobedience as a 'mistake as big as the Himalayas', because somewhere in India demonstrations in its wake were becoming violent.

Civil disobedience is not among the main forms of non-violent politics in Buddhism. The Buddhist non-violent movement has questioned the effectiveness of civil disobedience as a mere reaction to unjust action: anyone who remains caught up in the logic of action and reaction cannot free himself for peace-making. Therefore the struggle for harmony and reconciliation, the search for another perspective on problems, is in the foreground of Buddhist thought. However, in the Buddhist history of the twentieth century there have also been radical forms of violations of rules which come close to civil disobedience.

Since the 1980s a vigorous debate has broken out among Tibetan Buddhists who live in exile in India as to what role civil disobedience should play in the fight to free Tibet from Chinese domination and what forms are appropriate. Especially the younger generation, most of whom have grown up in exile, are increasingly discontented with the course of the Tibetan policy practised by the Dalai Lama. They expect decisive action, and attempt by their actions in particular to move the Indian government to take a harder line in negotiations with China. There have been hunger strikes by younger Tibetans in front of Indian government buildings, which are meant to back up the demands for a tougher foreign policy: since 1998 they have been broken up by the police; the hunger strikers are then forcibly put in hospitals. The Dalai Lama, who is attempting to persuade the Chinese government to fall in with Tibetan independence by negotiations at a diplomatic level, has been very restrained in commenting on such actions. He knows that the existence of Tibetan exiles' institutions in India depends on the benevolence of the Indian government.

Spending one's life in non-violent protest against injustice has a tradition in the Buddhist world. In 1967 the social worker Nhat Chi Mai immolated herself on the steps of a pagoda in Saigon to protest against the dictatorship in South Vietnam. With her action she followed the Buddhist *bodhisattva* ideal: sacrificing herself for the well-being of humankind and in so doing postponing her own redemption from the cycle of suffering existences.

Conflict and violence

'Only in a conflict does one recognize the violent, but one can speak of non-violence only where it would be natural and perhaps even justified to use violence, and then only when it solves the problems which normally are tackled with violence. In a conflict the non-violent do not seek to avoid the wrath of their opponents, to arouse their compassion, to trick them; rather, they try to reach agreement in complete clarity. In order to achieve this goal, depending on the situation, rough words can be as useful as gentle ones; one can just as easily use vigorous gestures which perplex people, sarcastic statements which shake them up, curses which warn them and in extreme cases even blows. Yes, even blows, provided that they are as free from violence as the amputation of a limb carried out by a surgeon for the purpose of healing.'

In this provocative statement the founder of L'Arche and

Catholic disciple of Gandhi, Lanza del Vasto (see pp. 141f.), draws attention to the close connection between non-violence and conflict. Non-violent action means engaging in and responding to conflicts in the personal, social and political sphere. At the same time he does away with the notion that the essential mark of non-violence is just being harmless, courteous, patient, yielding or friendly. He associates the presence of violence in a conflict with the motivation of those who act non-violently. As also in this statement of Lanza del Vasto, talk about conflicts, like the concrete means of dealing with them, is largely shaped by non-religious language, as long as it is a question of techniques and methods of transforming the conflict. Nevertheless, behind the decisions to take a particular course are not only pragmatic considerations but also religious motivation and ethical insights.

The Cambodian monk Maha Ghosananda writes that 'the ultimate causes and conditions of all conflicts lie in our spirit'. From the Buddhist perspective it is necessary to tone down the factors which lead to conflict, overcoming the 'separation of the self' by greater consciousness and heightened attentiveness towards one's own motives and feelings. For the separation of the self, which rates one's own needs, interests and values more highly than those of others, is a decisive psychological factor in the origin of suffering, the ending of which is the goal of the Buddhist doctrine of redemption.

Nevertheless, Buddhist thought and practice have also concerned themselves with measures which make it possible to deal with conflicts which arise already on the way to redemption. The North American Theravada monk Santikaro spells out his Thai teacher Buddhadhasa's vision of a society whose longing is stilled, a *nibbana* society. In this way he explains how in the suffering existence of a social being like man, conditions can be created for removing the obstacles to inner growth and furthering the development of spiritual awareness. Among other things he explains the third principle of the 'Noble Eightfold Path', right speech, as correct communication: 'First of all we must develop channels and methods of communication by means of which our "Groups for Buddhist Practice" can come to an understanding with one another in an honest, friendly, effective and useful way and at an appropriate time . . . That also means that we should ensure that there is sustained discussion in our groups, that we should allow all voices to be heard, and not suppress the views, opinions and sensibilities of others.'

The Thai social critic Sulak Sivarska points out that conflicts can open up changes and that – whatever the outcome – they contain the possibility of learning more about oneself and others. According to Sivarska, Buddhism creates the philosophical presupposition for putting the point of dispute of a conflict in another context: 'If we have learned basically that everything is transitory, we can simply change events by seeing them differently. We have the power to change our disputes into peace, an art which needs a particular skill. The expression "skill with means" (*upaya*) is very important in Buddhism and designates this very process.' As a presupposition for this it is necessary to be aware of one's own motives, to recognize anger and offence and to develop understanding and compassion. 'We need concentration and attentiveness for the Buddhist attitude to the resolution of conflicts.'

Buddhists like Maha Ghosananda have played an important role in efforts to mediate in international conflicts. The capacity to observe one's own role and emotions is something that Western mediators are also attempting to develop. For this reason there is much reflection in such circles on Buddhist experiences communicated by monks like Thich Nhat Hanh.

The Christian theologian Dorothee Sölle has divided violence into violence from below, violence from above and violence from within. By the last form she means 'the acceptance of violence, becoming accustomed to violence as the norm'. She describes how violence from above, i.e. generally accepted economic and military violence, strives to become violence from within. That leads to only part of the violent relations being perceived in public discussion, the violence from below, for example that of young people who socially have no power or perspective. This violence is abhorred, whereas people submit to violence from above without putting it in question.

A fundamental debate on the use of violence, in which ideas familiar from Dietrich Bonhoeffer are also echoed, took place between the Nicaraguan priest and revolutionary Ernesto Cardenal and the US peace activist Daniel Berrigan. In an interview in 1977 Cardenal said: 'The real revolutionary is an enemy of violence; he wants life and not death. But it can happen that the revolution has to be violent. Sometimes it must use violence because those in power do not yield power voluntarily, in other words, do not give in to the people. And this violence is completely justified. It is the right to resist, which even the church has always allowed all people. By that I do not mean the concept of the "just war"; perhaps there can be no such thing today.'

Daniel Berrigan opposes this regrettable profession of violence and calls it baneful simply 'in a world which is confused and fascinated by the myth of simplifications and final solutions to change front and take up arms'. He does not believe that this violence creates a juster society, even if now it comes from the left. 'In this bloody century our religion has little to offer, little that is not poisoned or broken or misused. But we have one thing: our refusal to direct bombs or rifles against the bodies of our brothers and sisters, whom we persistently call brothers and sisters, even if a state delighting in war or a church which blesses war wants to drive us into enmity against them.'

'Call men to the path of your Lord with wisdom and kindly exhortation. Reason with them in the most courteous manner,' is a verse from the Qur'an (16, 125) which makes a statement about enduring conflict and refers to constructive methods. However, alongside it also stand statements which can be used to justify the use of violence. If, as Mohammed Arkoun and Farid Esack propose, the Qur'an is understood as an existential word, then the Muslim non-violent movement must grapple with the question of which tradition it wants to adopt. Fatima Mernissi has pointed out that there are only a few places today where this process is possible. The existence of dictatorial regimes, economic pressures and the ideologizing of Islam by movements which make religion mythology or its language a political slogan present obstacles to this process which are difficult to overcome.

Economics and social justice

'Whereas materialists are primarily concerned with possessions, Buddhists are primarily concerned with liberation. But Buddhism is "the middle way" and therefore it by no means has a hostile attitude to physical well-being. It is not riches that stand in the way of liberation but being tied to them; it is not a delight in pleasant things that stands in the way of liberation but a longing for them. Therefore the basic notion of Buddhist economic theory is simplicity and non-violence. From the standpoint of an economist, the miracle of the Buddhist way of life lies in the extreme rationality of its pattern – amazingly small means lead to utterly satisfying results.'

In his classic book *Small is Beautiful*, Ernst Friedrich Schumacher points out that no economics is independent of basic assumptions and therefore societies which strive for a Buddhist way of living should also have an economy with a Buddhist stamp. The Noble Eightfold Path's principle of 'right means of livelihood' aimed at the removal of suffering therefore provides points of contact. Instead of this, though, Schumacher argues, Asian economists and politicians are imitating Western models of development. He comes to the conclusion that a Buddhist-style economy is achieved in small local communities with a high degree of self-sufficiency which are less open to violence than those which are involved in a world-wide trade system. 'The most favourable pattern of consumption, in which a high degree of satisfaction is produced by a comparatively small number of commodities, allows a person to live without great pressure and great tension.'

In Asia Schumacher, who travelled in India and Burma and worked as an economic adviser there, did not always meet with great understanding of his thoughts. However, they are very popular in the non-violent movements of India and South-East Asia. Many of Schumacher's ideas are echoed in particular by the Thai social critic Sulak Sivarska, who put in question the orientation of modern models of development on consumption. These ideas bear much resemblance to Buddhadasa's understanding of a society orientated on *dhamma* (right, correct doctrine, truth).

In Sri Lanka, the practice of the Buddhist non-violent movement has produced the Sarvodaya movement of the former teacher A.T. Ariyaratne. He began in 1958 with work camps in impoverished and neglected villages on the island in which he started village-awakening work – Ariyaratne understands Sarvodaya to mean 'the awakening of all'. So this is development work which not only derives its successes from the transfer of technology but also attaches importance to the social, cultural, personal and spiritual level and also the form of the economy. The initiative, which so far has been able to mobilize a great many people, consists in motivating the rural population themselves to become involved in the necessary development work instead of making them the objects of a process which they do not determine. The most important principle is *shramadana*, literally the free gift of labour. This links up with the Buddhist concept of generous giving (*dana*), one of the 'ferries' to perfection with which generosity is practised. Hitherto in Sri Lanka *dana* was understood as giving alms to the orders of Buddhist monks. Through *shramadana* the movement has adapted this concept for itself and applied it to work for the common good.

The interconfessional organization Satyodaya ('Awakening to the Truth'), founded by Catholics, and the projects of the Sri Bodhiraja Foundation in Embilipitiya in the south of the island, founded by Buddhist monks, work on similar principles. The Buddha had founded the *sangha* (monastic orders) 'for the well-being of the many, the happiness of the many', and had sent out the monks into the world. In the first period of Buddhism this included social and constructive initiatives – the monks in the foundation in Embilipitya are taking this up again. With this temple project the monk Omalpe Sobhita, who himself comes from a very poor family but was able to study in Sri Lanka and India and get to know other Buddhist ideas in South-East Asia, and who is now organizing environmental education on behalf of the United Nations in Cambodia, attempted to do away with the separation of spiritual and material responsibility. His aim, also in dealing with threats and military violence directed against local rebellions in the 1980s, and with large industries which destroy the environment, is the creation of social harmony through a persistent, critical dialogue.

The Indian Gandhian and economist J.C. Kumarappa also investigated the possibility of sustained decentralized develop-ment which strengthens the village economies and takes all human needs seriously. His approach goes back to Gandhi, who regarded the economic independence of India, indeed of the whole population of the land, as a presupposition for real inde-pendence. In his view, an essential element of this is the appropri-ation of production by small local units and the consumption of commodities which have been produced as locally as possible. 'The rebirth of the village is possible only if it is no longer exploited. Mass industrialization must necessarily lead to direct or indirect exploitation of the inhabitants of the villages, because then the problems of competition and the domination of the market emerge. We must concentrate our attention on making sure that the village looks after everything itself and produces mainly for its own use.'

The movement, which refers back to Gandhi's teaching, therefore propagated the manufacture, distribution and wearing of *khadi*, i.e. hand-spun and hand-woven material. However, the movement only began to change society through the land-gift and village-gift campaigns of Vinoba Bhave after the 1950s. Vinoba called land-gift *bhumidana yagna*, sacrifice through the gift of land, and thus gave the spiritual terms *dana* (see above) and *yagna* (sacrificial action) new meaning. By village-gift (Hindi *gramdana*) he then understood further development, the voluntary collectivization of the use of the land and the creation of communal institutions.

In 1982 in Bombay, Achhyut Deshpande, for many years a colleague of Vinoba, who died in May 1998, initiated a symbolic blockade of the greatest abattoir in Asia. By this action the activists wanted to point out that the protection of the Indian population of cattle and buffaloes by legislation is not sufficient, given the mechanisms of the market. The slaughter of young cattle is allowed only in exceptional cases, but this law is regularly flouted as a result of corruption. The abattoir produces meat for export, above all to the rich oil-producing countries, and in so doing contributes to the destruction of the cattle stock in India. Cattle play a major role in the rural economy as draught animals, as milk-producers appropriate to local conditions, and as part of an agricultural economy which aims at subsistence or above all local production. The blockade in Bombay, which was regularly removed by the police, brings out the connection between the interests of a trade system incorporated into the liberal world economy and the impoverishment of the Indian population. Here it makes use of the respect that cows enjoy in the Indian tradition: the movement calls itself the 'Cow Protection Movement'. However, it runs the risk of playing into the hands of radical Hindus who have inscribed the myth of the cow on their banners and in this way take action against non-Hindu minorities. Therefore at an early stage the Gandhian Cow Protection Movement sought dialogue with the predominantly Muslim abattoir workers and not only described its aims with Hindu symbolism but also investigated evidence from Islamic history to see what role was attributed to cattle. Though the accents are different, there too there are statements which describe the paramount significance of cattle for the development of the rural economy.

In Islam the secular and religious spheres are not thought of separately. Therefore economic and social life is traditionally the centre of attention for religious Muslims, on the same footing as personal and spiritual life. The prohibition of interest on loans and the tax on the poor – two important religious duties in Islam – are an expression of a concern for social justice. However, giving more than what was prescribed as an offering for the poor and disadvantaged was always an action which was highly respected in Islamic history. In Pakistan, Abdul Sattar Edhi and Akhter Hameed Khan are known for their Islamic humanism, which is combined with a mystical world-view. In the metropolis of Karachi in South Pakistan, Edhi has built up a system of basic health institutions which have been established through private giving and the collaboration of voluntary helpers, independently of state institutions.

At the age of sixty-five, the writer and historian Hameed Khan began to build up a social infrastructure in a poor district: a drainage system, a health service, schools, educational programmes for women and children and literacy campaigns were all created – and not least jobs. Like Edhi, Hameed Khan is exposed to the criticism of the Muslim groups and parties struggling for power. For he is concerned not with party politics but with self-help, the involvement of the population of the task of creating its own institutions in a local framework.

A thought of the Persian mystic Sa'adi was motivation for the

Iranian social worker and founder of a school for social work, Sattareh Farman Farmaian, to devote herself to the disadvantaged in society: 'People are like parts of a body which is created from the same substance; if a part is hurt and in pain, then the rest cannot remain in peace and quiet. If the distress of others leaves you un-involved, then you cannot be called a human being.' Her commit-ment, too, was not recognized by the Islamic government: after the Iranian revolution Farmian was arrested, and although she was acquitted, she had to go into exile.

A clash involving non-violent techniques and strategies took place in the Christian liberation theology of Brazil during the conflicts between the big landowners and the peasants over land. Hildegard Goss-Mayr, Jean Goss and those working for the human rights and non-violent organization Servicio Paz y Justicia (see p. 29) supported communities of tenants or landless agricul-tural workers with their knowledge about the foundations of Christian non-violence so that they could deal effectively with confiscation, expulsion and the direct use of armed force. Arch-bishop Dom José Maria Pires, who played a part in the non-violent fight of peasants in the state of Paraíba in north-west Brazil, wrote in 1978: 'To read the gospel in a book is very good. But if one sees it realized in life, in work, in the struggles and in the unity of our brothers, it lightens the way better and warms people's hearts more strongly.'

Hildegard Goss-Mayr expects the churches 'to go beyond char-itable development aid that is needed and commit Christians to the establishment of just economic relations for poor peoples'. The ecumenical initiative for the Jubilee Year 2000, which was very prominent in the closing years of the twentieth century, based on the biblical 'year of jubilee' in which debts were written off, has been an important campaign calling for the cancellation of debt for the economically weak countries of Africa, Asia and Latin America.

Environment and nature

'Allah has given us the earth in trust, as *amanah*. It cannot sustain the kind of progress that capitalism and the consumer society have adopted.' In saying this, Farid Esack sums up the Muslim attitude to the environment. In his view human beings are the stewards and users of nature, but they also have to protect it in accordance with God's commands. Esack and other Muslim thinkers of the South emphasize that human beings will not do justice to this responsibility if they follow the development model of European and North American industrial societies. But no non-violent approach to problems of the environment has come into being in Buddhism beyond these efforts.

In the Buddhist world, too, actions to protect the environment are still relatively new. The Thai monk Phra Prachak Khuttacitto has become known for opposing the interests of the wood industry, which is supported by the military. For fifteen years he travelled through Thailand as a forest monk, meditated and studied Buddhist doctrine. After he had settled in a temple in the north-east of Thailand in 1989, his experiences led him to regard the protection of the forests as also being a protection of Buddhism.

Phra Prachak, who managed to secure the support of the village for his concern to preserve one of the last forests in the country, began to perform on trees the ceremonies prescribed for the ordination of Buddhist monks. Traditionally yellow robes are bound round holy trees to show respect and to protect them. Prachak adopted the symbol and consecrated all the great trees of the forest. In a further ceremony a consecrated white cord which is normally put round the wrist of believers was put round the forest. On such occasions Prachak instructed the population on the value of the trees for the ecology and economy of the land. Prachak was threatened and attacked by local soldiers for his commitment; his temple was fired on and finally destroyed; and on several occasions he himself was arrested and put on trial. Senior monks in his home region disapproved of his actions and withdrew support from him; the inhabitants of villages yielded to attempts at intimidation and gave up contact with him. In 1994 Prachak, who could no longer stand the pressure, gave up his robes and returned to the lay state under the name Prachak Pethsingha.

Prachak belonged to the Sekhiyadhamma group, Thai monks concerned with the preservation of nature and social development. This group is inspired by the ideas of the Theravada monk and reformer Buddhadasa, who died in 1993. Starting from his thought, the monk Santikaro Bhikkhu, who comes from Chicago and lived for ten years with Buddhadasa in south Thailand, as his disciple and translator refers to the Noble Eightfold Path of Buddhist teaching and expands it so that it becomes a 'Noble Social Path'. He divides the fifth principle of *samma ajiva*, 'right means of livelihood', into 'right economy' and 'right ecology'. He wants ecological action to be governed by a communal control of the resources of a region, because rural communities usually have their own interest in the preservation of the basis of their life. There should be community forests around the fields administered and cultivated by the communities, and between them nature reserves to preserve the variety of species. 'The consecration of trees, the establishment of "Buddha circles" (*Buddha mandala*), "Buddha fields" (*Buddha kheta*), the revival of the tradition of freeing and feeding animals, taking children along for "forest processions" (*tudong*) and the holding of meditation vigils – all this can contribute to protecting these places and the beings which live there.'

Buddhadasa himself went beyond the protection of the environment with the aim of preserving it for present and future generations. Linking a Thai word with a Pali term, he calls nature *dhamma-jati*, i.e. what proceeds from *dhamma* (the right teaching, the natural law). This means that according to Buddhadasa the protection of nature is the expression of an unselfish and sensitive attitude towards nature which does not serve a purpose defined by human beings.

Hindu popular religion knows many traditions, the deeper sense of which lies in the preservation of the natural environment along with controlled use of it by the local population. Sacred trees and sacred hedges are known throughout India. Rivers are worshipped as deities. Rites which regulate incursions on nature reserves such as the Valley of Flowers in the Himalayas time and again make it clear to people that human beings and nature are inseparable elements of a system.

The Indian movement for protecting trees, called the Chipko movement after the Hindi word for 'cling to, embrace', has made use of these traditional symbols and given them a new definition in keeping with present-day facts: 'Brothers, this forest is our home. We get healing plants and vegetables from it. Do not cut down the forest. If you cut down the forest this mountain will fall on our village, the flood will come, the winter fields will be washed away – brothers, do not destroy our home.' Gaura Devi, who was fifty years old at the time, made these remarks to forestry workers who despite protests had been sent to cut down the forest behind the remote mountain village of Reni. The women under her leadership opposed the workers and despite threats stood firm, so the forest could finally be saved.

The Hindu activist Sunderlal Bahuguna combined the non-violent movement with yet another tradition by making a link with an event in the desert state of Rajasthan in 1730. At that time, according to the tradition of the Bishnoi cult, women under the leadership of Amrita Devi had resisted the clearing of a holy forest by clinging to trees and not giving way even to the axes of the forestry workers. The symbolism of the Chipko movement once again took up this unprecedented event, even if no trees in the Himalayas were actually saved by clinging to them.

Other movements in India which seek to protect the environment with non-violent action and to make a constructive contribution to non-violent forms of life are the movements for saving river valleys in the face of gigantic dam projects and for opposing the development of the nuclear industry.

Christian approaches to the protection of the environment refer today to the origins of the churches' Conciliar Process for Justice, Peace and the Preservation of Creation, which was formulated at the Sixth General Assembly of the World Council of Churches in Vancouver in 1983.

The Vancouver Declaration was accepted enthusiastically and put into practice at a variety of levels. Not least, various groups and organizations concerned about the increasing spread of the gene technology industry have taken up its ideas. The question how creation can be preserved if human beings become the creator has found great resonance with groups concerned with the ethical, economic and ecological problems of this branch of industry.

Another area in which many Christians have been involved with non-violent action has been the protest against the nuclear industry. In Great Britain Christians were prominent for many years in the Aldermaston marches organized by CND, and in Germany more recently in 1985 and 1988 on a 'crusade for creation' Christians carried large wooden crosses on their shoulders from locations of the nuclear industry to the nuclear centre at Gorleben. 'A concern for the preservation of creation, the continued construction of nuclear sites in Gorleben, the clashes on the roads, and the confrontation which was increasing in radicalism and violence, led a group of Christians to seek a way which had something just as radical from the Christian perspective to set against this violent radicalism. Their radicalism consists in non-violence, but also in clear partisan support for the weak, for the damaged creation.'

Food and lifestyle

'The longer I am a vegetarian, the more I feel how wrong it is to kill and eat animals. I believe that the consumption of meat and fish is a denial of all ideals, even of all religions. How can we ask God for mercy if we ourselves have no mercy? As long as people shed the blood of innocent creatures, there can be no peace, no freedom, no harmony between people. Slaughter and righteousness cannot dwell together.'

These words of the Jewish writer Isaac Bashevis Singer express the attitude of many Jewish vegetarians. The American mathematician Richard H.Schwarz, who is a champion of a vegetarian lifestyle, refers to the Old Testament tradition to demonstrate that the Jewish religion always favoured a meatless diet and allowed the consumption of flesh only on certain conditions and out of necessity, to some degree as a concession to human weakness. He can refer to statements by the rabbi Abraham Isaac Kook, who as chief rabbi before the foundation of Israel stated that the Jewish food laws were meant to lead people to become vegetarians, for in the future messianic age everyone would be vegetarian. He said that the prophecy of Isaiah that 'the wolf will lie down with the lamb and the leopard with the kid' (11.6–9) indicated this.

The reasons for a vegetarian lifestyle in the spirit of religious laws, as advocated by Schwarz and by Christian supporters of a vegetarian lifestyle in Europe and North America, are:

– Eating meat goes against the commandment not to kill, which also applies to killing animals (*religious and moral argument*);
– The eating of meat is less healthy than a meatless diet and thus goes against the obligation to keep one's own body healthy (*medical argument*);

- Animal production goes against the commandment to deal prudently and responsibility with animals as part of creation (*ethical argument*);
- Animal production costs far more in resources than the production of grain and vegetables (*ecological argument*);
- Animal production wastes resources which are lost to people in regions which suffer from a lack of food (*economic argument*).

Whereas the religious and moral and the ethical arguments have long been motivation for Christian vegetarians in Europe (for example, Tolstoy), from the beginning of the 1980s a Christian solidarity movement has increasingly been concerned with North-South questions and has referred in particular to the ecological and economic arguments. This has had a considerable impact on public awareness.

In general a vegetarian lifestyle is often associated with Asian cultures. Thus Gandhi's disciple Vinoba Bhave sees renunciation of eating meat as the goal of Hindu culture, as a meritorious result of the self-control of earlier generations. Today, since many millions of Hindus are vegetarians, the abandonment of the consumption of milk products should be the object of concerns for a developed lifestyle. However, Bhave adds that it is not the choice of food that is decisive, but the amount that anyone consumes.

In general it becomes clear from a survey of the works of the classics of non-violent thought and action that meatless eating is not usually at the centre of interest and efforts, as today in many circles in Central Europe, where this is regarded as a possible way of changing something in oneself. Even Mahatma Gandhi, who came from a Hindu community which rejected the eating of meat and who during his study in England came into contact with vegetarians and became a convinced vegetarian, had other priorities. Gandhi, who in his ashrams imposed a simple meatless diet, wrote this about the relationship between *ahimsa* (non-violence) and vegetarian food: '*Ahimsa* is not a matter of diet; it goes beyond that . . . Restraint in the choice of food is to be recommended, is even necessary, but it touches only the hem of *ahimsa*. People can allow themselves a wide range in matters of diet and yet be a personification of *ahimsa* and command our respect if their hearts overflow with love and assuage the sorrow of others and are purged of all passions. On the other hand, a*himsa* is extremely strange in someone who is always excessively anxious about matters of diet, and he is a miserable poor devil if he is a slave of his selfishness and passions and hard of heart.' Gandhi regarded control of one's own needs as a presupposition of spiritual power.

The South African writer and activist Farid Esack refers to more fundamental problems when he cites the Muslim regulation about cleanness in relation to food and says that a responsible attitude today means more than looking to see whether food is *halal*. It is necessary 'to ask where the money for it ends up'. He thinks that only a lifestyle which emphasizes the intention of having less is compatible with Islam. There is no other way if famine and the destruction of the environment are not to be implanted – the Muslim system of values prefers living beings to material things.

Thus like Leo Tolstoy, Gandhi and Vinoba chose a simple ascetic life and attempted to produce themselves the products that they needed to live on. Gandhi derived the recognition that the life of a farmer and a craftsman are the true life from reading a book by Ruskin (see above, p. 85). His choice of a simple lifestyle was also a sign of solidarity with the wide range of people in India with whom he identified himself. Like Gandhi, the Sicilian activist Danilo Dolci also decided for a life of poverty in order to win the trust of the oppressed population of the island. But here it was by no means a romantic transfiguration of the simple peasant life with all its hindrances.

In their fifth vow, on poverty, the co-founders of the L'Arche communities in France which have been established since 1948 by Gandhi's disciple Lanza del Vasto promise one another 'to live simply, moderately and purely and to love poverty, in order in this way to progress constantly on the way of denial and mercy'. Lanza del Vasto, who had studied Christian mediaeval traditions, saw work as spiritual nourishment. At the same time he emphasized 'the voluntary acceptance of work as a rule of decency and a conscientious duty. Here the first step should be taken by those who benefit from the existing system.' It also become clear at this point why a simple lifestyle and vegetarian food were not among the main demands of those who fought non-violently for justice and liberation: there was too great a danger that this would legitimate an unjust system. For example, Martin Luther King protested about the wretched state of the workers in the USA, Dolci about the hunger of the Sicilian children.

The Buddhist representatives of the non-violent movements also put their priorities here. The Thai activist Sulak Sivarska makes a similar comment on the first Buddhist vow, not to kill a living being, to the remarks of the Muslim Esack: 'In the mass production of meat is there still respect for the life of the animals? If people in the countries in which meat is eaten were to take action against animals being bred as food, then that would show compassion not only towards the animals but also towards the people who live in poverty and need grain to survive.' In his writings he criticizes a consumer-orientated lifestyle as opposed to Buddhist thought. It is contrary to Asian values in general and Buddhist ideas in particular for individual personal advantage to be aimed at through competition, and for consumerism to become blatant.

Hildegard Goss-Mayr sees signs of hope in a change in Western societies which are above all the object of the criticism of the non-violent movements of Africa, Asia and Latin America. For them, 'the mode of being of poverty', the realization of the kingdom of God in human beings, stands over against the 'mode of being of having', of wanting to possess everything, including God. This includes a restriction on the commodities which accrue to one as a proportion of the resources at the disposal of the entire population of the world and the choice of a simple lifestyle. The Latin-

American churches which have developed the theology of liberation, many Christian grass-roots initiatives in Central Europe, and people who are working at the development of a *shalom* diaconate, are challenging the official churches to reorientate themselves in this direction.

A further characteristic of the Western lifestyle becomes the focus of criticism: the Vietnamese Buddhist Thich Nhat Hanh, the South African Muslim Farid Esack and the North American Trappist Thomas Merton shed light on the haste and hectic nature of our time. Merton emphasizes that activism, prescribing a number of projects for oneself, destroys 'the inner capacity for peace'. Esack observes in the model of the Prophet Muhammad the claim to become a complete person who encounters others as a human being and not as an 'activity machine'. In order to regain this strength to meet others and give them his full attention, the Prophet withdrew from the public from time to time. Thich Nhat Hanh believes that this hectic way of life is the result of an alienation from ourselves. In order to heal ourselves and the society around us it is necessary to practise mind control and to make contact with 'the seed of peace, contentment and happiness in us'.

Peace churches and religious peace communities

As a state religion in the Roman empire, from the fourth century on Christianity had a close connection with the power of the state. And it was according to the principle 'whose territory, his religion' (Latin *cuius regio, eius religio*) that from the Thirty Years' War onwards the German rulers acted. As early as the sixteenth century the Reformers – especially Martin Luther – provided theological justification for the rulers' claim to power. Clearly dissociating themselves from this alliance with the political authorities, smaller religious groups, the so-called 'Anabaptists', adopted other courses. And what had already happened to the religious deviants in previous centuries who had been persecuted as 'heretics' also happened to them: because of their principles, their insistence on a deliberate decision for baptism and rejection of any armed service of the state, they suffered bloody persecution from the rulers and the church authorities. They survived only in the regions of rulers who were well disposed towards them or by emigrating to Poland, Russia and North America. These 'peace churches' included the Quakers, the Mennonites and the Brethren Communities.

Since their origin, in seventeenth-century England, the Quakers, really the 'Religious Society of Friends', have consistently stood for non-violence and equal rights in all spheres of life. Because of hostility towards them, some Quakers emigrated to North America, where they sold on again the land of the original population of North America which had been transferred to them by the English king. In contrast to other immigrants, they rejected armed protection of their settlements. To a considerable degree, within their communities they also achieved equal rights and the abolition of hierarchies. In the eighteenth and nineteenth centuries the Quakers of North America engaged resolutely in public action against any form of slavery and played a key role in its abolition. Moreover they founded social welfare organizations as peace initiatives.

The Quakers are especially active through their Quaker Peace and Service Organization based in London. All over the world they support local initiatives for peace, especially in communities torn by ethnic conflicts. Some Quakers, like the Englishman Adam Curle, have achieved a tremendous amount by unofficial mediation in political conflicts at the international level.

In 1957 the peace churches of the Brethren and the Mennonites founded the International Fellowship of Reconciliation, and other European Christians, initially under the aegis of the World Council of Churches in Geneva, founded the Christian peace service EIRENE, which as an ecumenical organization is still involved in non-violent projects in Europe, Africa, and North and Latin America. EIRENE names and analyses the violence that is directly and manifestly present, but also structural violence, and practises solidarity in partnership with the people in the South who are attempted to overcome the consequences of colonialism. In order to emphasize the connection between the wealth in the North and the distress in the South, EIRENE volunteers are also active among the marginal groups of industrialized societies.

The peace work of the Protestant communities is now matched by two important Catholic movements, the 'houses of hospitality' established by Dorothy Day's Catholic Workers Movement in the USA and the L'Arche communities of the Italian Lanza del Vasto. Both have their origin in the 1930s.

As we saw, after the publication of her journal *The Catholic Worker* on May Day 1933, the flood of homeless led Dorothy Day, an ex-Communist converted to the Catholic faith, to open up her house in order to practise what she and the French thinker Peter Maurin had worked for in journalism. This led to the first 'houses of hospitality' in US cities. Peter Maurin likewise developed Catholic Workers Communities in the country, which began to live out a socialism with a Catholic stamp. Maurin's motto was: 'Build a new community within the empty old one' (cf. also pp. 24f.).

The Sicilian Lanza del Vasto visited Mahatma Gandhi in his ashram in India in 1936. Deeply impressed, after three months he returned to Europe, there to found an ashram which would combine the Indian institution with Christian thought in a way suitable to the social situation in Europe. Delayed by the war, the first L'Arche community was formed in the south of France in 1948. A 'working order' orientated on non-violent principles, Arche has partly taken up traditions of the Catholic religious orders, like the hierarchical patriarchal organization and the long process of incorporating new members into the community. However, men and women who live together individually or as families can be members of L'Arche. During the Algerian war the L'Arche communities went public in France to act against the maltreatment of interned Algerians, to support conscientious objectors and also to hide them from the grips of the authorities. Moreover they took a stand against nuclear energy and against a military training ground on the Larzac plateau. The members of the L'Arche community promise in their common prayers to work, to be obedient, to take responsibility, to be concerned for purity, to love poverty, and to practise truthfulness and non-violence.

Mahatma Gandhi's ashram with its eleven vows repeated at every prayer time, which addresses similar options to those of Lanza del Vasto, was the inspiration for the Catholic L'Arche communities. Already in South Africa Gandhi was drawn into fellowship with other Indians in order to be able to offer protection and support to families when *satyagrahis*, those activists engaged in civil disobedience, were arrested. After his return to India he developed the traditional concept of the ashram in this direction. From of old in India spiritual teachers had lived with their disciples in communities which were partially self-supporting and which also assumed social tasks. Gandhi, for whom spiritual development was more important than his experiments at a political level, adopted this pattern and made his ashrams cells of resistance against the colonial government, and also laboratories for a new society. Vinoba Bhave in particular developed these notions, and on his travels on foot through India founded ashrams in several places which still combine a life orientated on spiritual principles with constructive projects for the disadvantaged of society. Simple life, a striving for self-sufficiency, a day divided by prayer meetings and communal activities, communal meals, physical work and crafts, the abolition of the barriers of caste, equal rights for men and women, the value attached to study, religious tolerance and critical reflection on the social and political situation still characterize most ashrams even today.

The Jewish kibbutz movement and the departure of the Muslim

Sufi orders from North African society on the model of Muhammad's departure from Mecca are two models which have much in common with the communities described. The attempt to form a cell for a new society, to live out utopian forms of life even in the present, and to fill traditional forms of religious practice with new revolutionary content – all these are also reflected in these movements. But both the Israeli kibbutzim and the mystical orders in Islam have resorted to armed force in their struggle with threats from outside. An interesting attempt to meet the Jewish and Arab challenges of peace work came about in Israel in 1972: very near to Jerusalem, Jews and Palestinians built the village Neve Shalom/Wahat as-Salam, 'Oasis of Peace'. On a plot of land rented from a nearby Trappist monastery families of both groups settled in equal numbers and began to create common structures. The school in which the children of both cultures are instructed in their own tradition, but in which knowledge of and respect for the other tradition is communicated, is particularly remarkable. That can be very difficult on official feast days, because the history of suffering of the one side is often linked with the feast days of the other. Together the groups also run a peace school which with the help of its now developed educational scheme organizes encounter seminars with Israeli and Palestinian groups (or mixed groups). Granted, there is a house of silence as the spiritual centre of the village, but no communal practice has developed there. In the process of communal life and daily discussion many inhabitants of Neve Shalom/Wahat as-Salam again become more aware of their own roots. Therefore they go their own ways in their spiritual life.

Initiatives like these, with all their limitations, are necessary in order to remind established institutions of the great religions of their task to make peace and to challenge them to conversion. Buddhist temples, in the tradition usually communities which are meant to be examples of a better society, have lost their influence in many countries of Theravada Buddhism. Only here and there is

reflection on the aims of the earliest Buddhist period: this is beginning in village temples in Thailand, Cambodia and Sri Lanka (see
pp. 158f.). In the south of France, as we have seen, the Vietnamese
Zen monk Thich Nhat Hanh has founded the meditation centre
Plum Village, a community in which Vietnamese, Europeans and
Americans live together and devote themselves to the practice of
mind control (see p. 110).

Saint Francis of Assisi is a model for peaceful action whose
influence extends far beyond the Catholic sphere. Gandhi intro-
duced the prayer for peace attributed to him into the daily canon
of prayer in his ashram. Nevertheless the Franciscans, like other
Catholic orders, only slowly became open to non-violent action.
Following the Second Vatican Council, in 1969 the Central
Franciscan Mission was formed in Bonn, which attempts to live
out the Franciscan message of non-violence at the present time.
For it mission means encouraging others – Christian and non-
Christian – by their action 'to make it possible to see and experi-
ence the kingdom of God on earth'.

Prison

For the brothers Philip and Daniel Berrigan in the USA, who on a
number of occasions from the end of the 1960s on went to prison
for their actions 'Swords into Ploughshares', the struggle for truth
and the public unmasking of the mendacity of US military policy
was the most important motivation. They burned draft papers for
the Vietnam war or invaded nuclear bases to do damage. Daniel
Berrigan gave two further reasons for this behaviour:

1. As older men we want to stand body and soul by the moral
   values which are expected by the young generation: 'They have

encountered in us the will to go with them into prison. We have put demands to them that we never hesitated to take on our own shoulders.'

2. Overcoming one's own selfishness: serving the community with one's own life. He compares life to good bread which is permeated with the powerful taste of yeast – a firm awareness of what is right. This awareness, this insight, should be shared by peace fighters taking upon themselves the restrictions of imprisonment.

A deep spirituality also plays a major role for the Berrigans (who otherwise 'really do not reflect much on these stays in prison', like most people who were prepared to go to prison for non-violent action). Their language is stamped by Christian symbolism. They did not attempt to avoid prison, but accepted it inwardly as part of their resistance.

Reflection on the significance of prison goes back to the American humanist David Henry Thoreau, whose views pointed the way for Martin Luther King, Mahatma Gandhi and many other committed people. 'Under a government which imprisons anyone unlawfully, prison is the appropriate place for a just person. The right place, the only place which Massachusetts has to offer today to its freer and less timid spirits, is prison, where they will be abandoned and excluded by the state, since they have already excluded themselves through their own principles.'

That statement was made by Thoreau 150 years ago in his famous essay 'On the Duty of Disobedience towards the State'. His words stand in contradiction to the widespread view that even now is still commonly held: those who go to prison are getting their just deserts. However, prison as a legally regulated form of punishment is also a consequence of civil disobedience which is already taken into account. Thoreau attracted attention and sensitized people against state injustice by his readiness to go to prison.

The motivation for accepting the withdrawal of freedom can

vary considerably. The Buddhist Aung San Suu Kyi, who lived for years under house arrest imposed by the Burmese generals, writes: 'In a system which denies the existence of fundamental human rights, fear tends to be the order of the day. Fear of arrest, fear of torture, fear of death, fear of losing friends, relatives, possessions, the means of earning a living; fear of poverty, fear of isolation, fear of failure. The worst form of fear is that which disguises itself as a sound mind or even as wisdom. It condemns the daily little courageous acts which help to preserve human self-respect and dignity, as stupid, frivolous, insignificant or useless.'

By her life Aung San Suu Kyi bears witness to what it means to overcome fear, to show that systems which despise humanity have no absolute power over people. She wants to offer encouragement to do what seems necessary in an unjust situation, but at the same time what is also possible in one's personal situation: 'But even under the most oppressive state machinery, time and again the courage develops, for fear is not the natural state of civilized people.' Aung San Suu Kyi is here referring to the Buddhist concept of *agati*, the four corruptions. One of these is *bhayagati*, corruption through fear, which also distracts people from other virtues.

For Mahadev Desai, Mahatma Gandhi's private secretary, his first thirteen-month stay in prison was in part an opportunity to reflect on himself, to prepare for years of resistance to the British colonial regime in India. In December 1921 he was convicted of having edited a banned newspaper. He had foreseen this in the leading article: 'It is probable that with all our colleagues and helpers we will be robbed of our slave-freedom. But life under falsehood, injustice and terror can be borne only in prison. Tyranny is powerful enough to control all the activities of our moral existence, but it cannot affect the immortal spirit. It may compel the former to submit to its law, but it cannot even dream of imposing its law on the latter.'

Mahadev saw prison as the expression of a greater freedom

which cannot be restricted by physical compulsion. He then suffered the humiliating conditions of imprisonment in the notorious prison of Allahabad. His struggle with suffering is documented and makes it clear that he sees himself challenged by it to overcome his own 'spiritual problems'.

Mahadev smuggled his first letter to Gandhi from prison. This impressed Gandhi as an illustration of the inhuman conditions of imprisonment in the prisons of the colonial regime, but he made the comment: 'I believe that the sending of this letter was a breach of prison discipline. In South Africa I always refused to respond to such letters. But in this case I regard Mahadev Desai's harmless breach of the regulations as forgivable.' In principle the Indian resistance fighters strictly observed the prison rules in order all the more effectively to be able to offer open and focussed resistance to laws which were identified as unjust. The regime could not accuse them of in any case only observing quite arbitrarily those laws which seemed to them to be opportune.

One event illustrates this. Two decades later the colonial administration wanted to keep secret the fact that Gandhi, his wife Kasturba, and Mahadev were in another prison, but a doctor wrote Kasturba's name on a prescription. Thereupon Mahadev pointed out to the official that the mistake would immediately have provoked public unrest in support of Gandhi, but the prisoners did not want this to happen through a mere mistake of the prison authorities.

Mahatma Gandhi grappled with Thoreau at an early stage and looked more closely at the motives for accepting imprisonment. He describes people engaged in *satyagraha* like this: 'A *satyagrahi* goes to prison not in order to bring confusion to the authorities but in order to convert them, by demonstrating his innocence to them. One should be clear that the readiness to go to prison without the necessary moral appropriation which *satyagraha* calls for is useless and in the end only leads to disillusionment.'

For Gandhi and Mahadev Desai, prison – in the later years

rather more comfortable than in Allahabad – was always also an occasion for turning inwards, for reflection, for rest in a battle for liberation which hardly ever offered them an occasion to withdraw, indeed often did not allow them sufficient sleep. So like Gandhi's most important disciple, Vinoba Bhave, they used their stays in prison to study, especially languages and classic literature.

Such power, and an awareness of the legitimacy of action, are needed for surviving prison sentences. In this way they become an effective public testimony: for someone willingly to allow his freedom to be taken away – even if only for a short time – does not leave either supporters or political opponents unaffected. Even in Western societies, where a fine or community service can often be substituted for prison, this is a clear sign. That is why the German Quaker activist Katja Tempel refused to accept a fine because she wanted to object to the verdict passed on her: with her 'loud as life' music demonstration against the nuclear centre in Gorleben in August 1994 she felt that she had not committed any breach of the law for which she now had to pay.

However, going to prison is different from martyrdom. While a prison sentence is served by the individual, the concern is shared by wider groups. Ultimately support is also necessary on a quite personal level. The Ploughshare activists around the Berrigan brothers or the South African Indians around the young Gandhi gathered in communities (see p. 146 above) in order to be able to look after members of the family in solidarity during their imprisonment. Involvement in a wider context of discussion makes it possible for others to go along with the individual personal decision to go to prison and elevates the transgression against the rules above the state of a mere criminal act, so that the injustice is shown up.

Reconciliation

The US Vietnam veteran Claude Thomas described his personal history of reconciliation like this: 'I was trained from birth to be a soldier, by the way I was brought up and the way I was encouraged . . . I was brought up only to obey authorities, no matter what authorities . . . At seventeen I went into the army and then to Vietnam . . . The character of my training was to learn to de-humanize the enemy. In this process of dehumanizing the enemy I myself became dehumanized.' In 1967 he was shot and severely wounded, and after spending nine months in hospital left the army at the age of twenty. There followed what today he calls the 'war after the war': violence, drugs, alcohol, prison. Only when he met the Vietnamese Zen monk Thich Nhat Hanh and visited a workshop for Vietnam veterans did his life begin to change. Thomas came into contact with Vietnamese, with himself, his feel-ings and hurts. He began to recall his childhood and all that had made him what he was. But he also began to live and to feel in the present.

The young couple Swati Desai and Michael Mazgaonkar live in a small village in the Indian state of Gujarat with the original local population in very simple conditions. They had the opportunity to finish their studies and could have made an urban career in India. Instead of this they live with people who are still outside the caste system and therefore suffer disadvantages by being excluded from many development programmes. Even develop-ment projects which have been begun in their region do them more harm than good because the projects are tailored to the needs of the urban population. Living with the tribal population puts Desai and Mazgaonkar in a position to identify economic and social problems and propose the beginning of solutions which further development and justice. They call their work, which draws on a spirituality based on Gandhi's non-violence, 'economic reconciliation', the attempt cautiously to restore justice in mutual relations and relations with society as a whole.

In December 1956 Martin Luther King ended the one-year bus boycott in Montgomery after the court decision to abolish racial segregation with a speech in which he advised caution: 'We have grown inwardly to such an extent through our experiences in this year of non-violent protest that a legal "victory" over our white brothers cannot satisfy us. We must show understanding for those who have oppressed us and also for what the Supreme Court has imposed on them. We must honestly recognize our own mistakes. We must act in such a way that it is possible for white and coloured people to live together in a real harmony of interests and under-standing . . . This is the moment when we must show quiet dignity and wise restraint . . . We must now move from protest to reconcili-ation. I am firmly convinced that God is at work in Montgomery.'

These three examples from different religious and social contexts show the broad spectrum in which reconciliation can take place. It is a process of healing during or at the end of conflicts. Reconcili-ation and peace act on each other. In Christian theology, recon-ciliation is closely connected with the death of Christ on the cross, reconciliation between humankind and God. For King, this relationship to God is manifested in reconciling action between people.

Processes of reconciliation comprise many steps which are sensitively tuned to each other: encounter and dialogue, the acknowledgment of guilt, the request for forgiveness, showing the truth, forgiveness, the doing of justice and attempts to overcome or change unjust structures. The presuppositions for successful reconciliation are empathy and courage, honest recollection of the past, honesty and patience, comfort and the offer of sorrow, repentance and the search for reparation. Reconciliation means forgiving but not forgetting. In particular the overcoming of silence and indifference by remembering is what first makes possible the healing of relationships and the restoration of community.

It is also important to recognize just how much time is needed for processes of reconciliation in some circumstances – sometimes generations. As reconciliation is both an individual and a social task, it is difficult to determine in conflicts in which the whole population had been involved when a process of reconciliation is completed. Reconciliation cannot be forced – it must happen voluntarily and calls for the decision of all the parties in the conflict to take part in it. There is no standard process for reconciliation. Every process of reconciliation has its own course and must be shaped by people who take full responsibility for their actions. Often there is a time lag in the processes of reconciliation: victims and perpetrators require different lengths of time and the need for reconciliation is stronger on the side of the perpetrators. But victims of violence also emphasize that they are seeking possibilities of reconciliation for their own healing and the restoration of their own dignity.

Rituals are necessary at some point in the process of reconciliation, often after a dispute has been settled. Religion offers traditional rituals of reconciliation or the framework for developing new rituals. For example, in her inaugural speech to the World Conference of Women in Beijing, the Burmese Aung San Suu Kyi describes the Buddhist *paravana* ceremony. In this ceremony at the end of the rainy season, the monks confess their transgressions and ask one another for forgiveness. She sees this as the precursor of a truth commission.

Alongside truth, justice is a precondition for successful reconciliation. The example of South Africa shows that sometimes both cannot be achieved to the same degree. In South Africa Desmond Tutu (see pp. 50–3) is President of the Truth and Reconciliation Commission which was set up in 1995. This commission works in three committees, one concerned with hearing victims of violations of human rights, one concerned with the question of compensation for victims and one concerned with amnesties for the perpetrators. Although on his appointment to the Commission Tutu said that the rehabilitation of the victims and the restoration of their dignity had priority in the work, it is the amnesty committee which has attracted the greatest attention.

This committee may grant immunity from prosecution to perpetrators who voluntarily accept offers of amnesty within a fixed period. To be granted it they must disclose all their crimes, name perpetrators, demonstrate political motives for the act and show that the orders were given by a political organization. But the immunity does not require repentance, a confession of guilt or reparation. This has provoked strong opposition from many victims and members of the public when senior police officers or apartheid officials describe their involvement in violations of human rights without any form of penitence but are then acquitted. Moreover the commission was completely overwhelmed by the further assertions of the many victims. A reparation for crimes in a society in which almost everyone took part in some form of political violence is almost impossible.

The Truth and Reconciliation Commission, which has been attacked from all sides with the aim of making it a political instrument, has managed to preserve its independence and take a first step towards national reconciliation. In the circumstances that was possible only because it excluded the quest for justice, in that perpetrators got off scot-free. For many victims that is hard to bear, but it is regarded as the price for a peace for which there was little leeway. For change in South Africa has not been brought about by the victory of one side but by negotiations. The old regime still had the military power and could hurl the country into chaos. However, most South Africans found quite intolerable a general amnesty which as in Chile simply forgets the crimes. As Tutu keeps emphasizing, that makes it all the more important to improve people's present economic situation. Without positive changes in the material sphere, in the long term there will also be no reconciliation.

Upbringing and education

In view of the problems of many former colonial societies, criticism of the appropriateness of a system of training with a Western orientation has led to answers from a Buddhist, Muslim and Hindu perspective.

For Mahatma Gandhi, the reform of the colonial system of education was an important part of the Indian fight for independence. But he regarded questions of upbringing as far more basic: 'By upbringing I mean the all-embracing formation of the best in the child and the human being – body, soul and spirit. The capacity to read and write is not the end of upbringing, nor even the beginning. It is merely one of the means by which man and woman can be brought up . . . I would therefore begin the upbringing of the child by teaching him a useful craft and enabling him to produce something from the moment that he begins on his exercises.' Elementary schools should contribute to their own support by production, but should also make this practical activity the object of investigations and discussions. Thus Gandhi's fellow workers and their children discussed political, social and economic questions through spinning cotton, calculated what they had achieved and developed their capacity to meditate or to be silent.

Gandhi had already made his first experiments in this direction in South Africa in his community called Tolstoy Farm. Certainly instruction in religious literature was also on the timetable, but the spiritual upbringing of the children was above all to be achieved through the example of the teachers: 'By spiritual development I understand the formation of the heart. A right development which is spiritual on all sides can take place only if it goes hand in hand with the upbringing of the bodily and the spiritual capacities of the child. They form an indivisible whole.' Gandhi regarded knowing the power of the soul, truth and love as more important goals of upbringing than literacy, a knowledge of facts or the knowledge of religious traditions and texts.

Gandhi's co-worker and disciple Vinoba Bhave, whose thought and action were stamped by a great knowledge of Hindu thought, stated in 1967 that education could not be limited to schools and universities: 'Learning and instruction are linked with every task. Any human task should be permeated with the atmosphere of study and performance.' To describe the role of the teacher Vinoba used the Sanskrit term *guru*, a spiritual leader who is asked by others for advice in questions about life, and *acharaya*, a teacher who has reflected well on his knowledge, who has time and again been concerned to make progress himself, and who has handed on what he knows. These concepts characterize the significance of the teachers in the ashram schools, the boarding-schools of the non-violent movement of India, and also in comparable projects of the Buddhist societies of South and South-East Asia.

Buddhist monks were traditionally the vehicles of education in their society, but they have largely been unable to adapt to the changed circumstances of modern times. However, because of the social crises in Thailand, many Thai monks have become active, influenced by the monastic reformer Buddhadasa Bhikkhu. One of them, Phra Rajvaramuni, declared that the main aim of education is to lead people to a life which they determine themselves, but that they also have to be shown the way to contribute together with others to a just and peaceful society. Rajvaramuni goes on to speak of the Buddhist principle of *kalayanamitta* ('virtuous, good, friend'), i.e. of learning through a good environment, the good company of others. The communication of wisdom here stands on an equal footing with the development of analytical thought. The children's village school of Kanchanaburi has adopted this principle since 1979; this is a self-supporting Buddhist community which is run on the same lines as the Indian ashram schools.

The development in Sri Lanka shows that while reflecting on religious values can be liberating, too much emphasis on them can be dangerous. The call for upbringing in indigenous Buddhist values, languages and traditions which was propagated after the independence of the island republic has encouraged the rise of nationalistic Sinhalese-Buddhist groups and ultimately laid the foundations for the civil war with the Tamil Hindu minority. Here the monastic orders have not served the majority population, which is becoming increasingly impoverished. In 1967, a young generation of Buddhist monks in Embilipitiya in the neglected south of Sri Lanka therefore began to put into practice Buddha's command to become active 'for the well-being of the many'. There were other projects, but educational projects came first in this work, which in addition to the traditional monastic teachings also comprised methods of social work.

At the beginning of the 1970s in Sicily Danilo Dolci (see pp. 141f.) initiated an educational programme with a Christian motivation which reacted to the local under-provision. In a relaxed atmosphere Dolci's co-workers tried out new possibilities of education with children, gave them access to other experiences of learning, and reinforced their capacities for group work and peaceful life together. In these experiments in the educational sector, Dolci, who is often compared with Gandhi, held firm to his vision of a juster society, for which he had to struggle with the Italian state, the Sicilian Mafia and the Catholic Church, which was interwoven with both.

Both Danilo Dolci and Mahatma Gandhi referred back to Leo Tolstoy (see above, p. 85), who in the 1860s on his estate in Yasnaya Polyana carried out the first educational experiments with the children of the rural population. For the Christian anarchist and mystic Tolstoy, upbringing had no defined goal. It served above all to free the individual for creative action in present-day society.

Tolstoy rejected any compulsion and any external discipline. In a situation in which chaos was understood as a natural state, Tolstoy expected much of the teacher: as one who was shaping children, the teacher was to listen more than tell, and then to change what he heard, put it in new contexts and develop it further.

Tolstoy also influenced Martin Buber, though he was never very creative in his educational practice, and A.S.Neill, the founder of Summerhill. Neill's experiments were discussed not only in the non-violent movements of Europe but also in India and Thailand, so that the children's village school of Kanchanaburi mentioned above drew on Neill's ideas as well as on Buddhist ideas.

Upbringing as understood by the non-violent reformers and revolutionaries mentioned above does not end when a person is grown up. Along with educationalists like the Brazilian Paulo Freire, Latin American liberation theologians keep emphasizing the importance of conscientization as a presupposition for social change. In his last pastoral letter before his murder, the Salvadorean archbishop Oscar Romero wrote: 'In the present social and political conditions of the country the evangelization of this people cannot content itself with continuing the tradition of a massive or purely moralizing preaching and instruction, but must emphasize an upbringing in the faith which furthers personality, which through small groups arouses the awareness of people so that they look at their environment critically in accordance with the criteria of the gospel.'

This is precisely what Martin Luther King put into practice when he instituted training for non-violent action in the church: 'In a series of meetings we trained the people in how they should behave. In front of the altar we put a row of chairs to represent the bus. At the head was the driver's seat. Then we chose a dozen "actors" and assigned each of them a role in a situation which they might possibly encounter. One man was the driver, the others were white and black passengers. In both groups there were courteous and hostile people. In the presence of the other members of the gathering the actors now played out a scene in which one passenger was insulted and hit . . . and at the end there was a discussion of all this.' As in the role-play in present-day training in non-violence, King and his fellow freedom-fighters practised how they would behave when provoked after the abolition of racial segregation. Training of this kind has its historical roots in the gatherings of the Society of Friends (Quakers).

Narayan Desai, the son of Gandhi's private secretary Mahadev Desai, gives a programmatic description of the relationship between non-violence and upbringing and sums it up like this: 'What is upbringing? It is the acceptance of the principle of non-violence in the development and furthering of human possibilities. What upbringing and education attempts to achieve in schools, non-violence attempts to achieve in society. It can be said that non-violence in the wider sense and in its purest application can hardly be distinguished from the upbringing of society. And from that follows the similarity of its methods.'

War and peace

'There is no consensus on the definition of a Christian approach to violence or non-violence. However, on the part of the churches there is a deep desire to create a permanent peace built on justice. The fact that many churches today have to grapple with the most varied forms of violence has given this desire a new urgency.' This 1997 statement by the World Council of Churches about its programme for the overcoming of violence is only one made by various church institutions and governments which are working for peace, responding to the prompting of organizations like the International Fellowship of Reconciliation and Service Civil International. These peace services have been active in local and regional peace work, in the work of reconciliation beyond the front lines in warring states, in reconstruction and refugee work, in training in non-violence in the sphere of humanitarian help, and in support of civil and non-violent resolution of conflicts. They work at the grass roots, with much personal commitment and few financial means. Their umbrella organizations like Pax Christi, and individual organizations like the International Fellowship of Reconciliation, attempt to influence the churches with their experiences and increasing notice is being taken of them. Their concept of peace is a dynamic one which aims at the creation of a positive peace and not just the abolition of war (cf. p. 49).

If the clash with Fascism and the Second World War were the focal points of the Christian peace services in the first post-war decades – say in reconciliation between Germany and France or between Germany and Poland – and later they concentrated on getting beyond the fronts in the Cold War and finally on the attempt to prevent nuclear rearmament in the 1980s, since the Gulf War in 1991 and the collapse of former Yugoslavia the aims have changed. Today concrete intervention in events, the support of social agents and the further developments of constructive methods of resolving civil conflicts stand in the foreground of their work. However, the Balkans war has also led to new discussions in these organizations about the justification for military intervention. The Catholic peace movement Pax Christi has most clearly made its theme the contradiction between the rejection of any form of violence, including military action with a view to peace, and an inability to provide rapid help without violence in the face of the suffering of the civil population. In general, non-violent positions have become established in these discussions, positions which point to the need for long-term action and identification of the military and political aims of an intervention by foreign armies which claims to be humanitarian. Nevertheless these organizations breathed again when the cease-fire in Bosnia in 1996 achieved by the military put an end to the immediate suffering. Sadly, church governments have been less clear on the matter of non-violence.

In the course of Christian history, time and again reference has been made to the option of the 'just war' which was formulated by Augustine at the beginning of the fifth century and by Thomas Aquinas in the thirteenth century. It is still discussed today, although as early as 1947 Cardinal Ottaviani, the Prefect of the Roman Congregation of Faith, declared that modern wars do not correspond to the conditions for a just and legitimate war. There can no longer be any ethical justification of war in a century of highly technological wars in which most victims are civilians and in which wars carry with them the possibility of bringing about the destruction of creation. Neither in the Gulf War nor in Bosnia were all other political means exhausted, and in neither of the two wars was there a defence with certain prospects of success. The issue was the political and economic interests of those who intervened.

Hildegard Goss-Mayr describes how the ideology of the just war has also moved the liberation theologians in Latin America. There the use of violence by the military was justified not with the argument of defence but with that of support for the poor and the oppressed. But the argument of Dom Helder Camara against this holds: 'Anyone who uses violence remains caught up in the spiral of violence; he does not break through the system of violence which dominates the world but feeds it and makes it escalate, in itself and in the war of liberation; he plants it in the new situation in a new form.' In an article on the 'theology of peace', written in 1997, Dorothee Sölle described how the military argument for a just war always runs the risk of becoming an argument for a holy war, if war is veiled with beautifying terms and describes as 'beneficial action'. This thought, says Sölle, has also found expression in secular talk about war. She hopes for peacemakers who take up the tradition of the discipleship of Christ in the earliest community and understand the Sermon on the Mount as words which shape reality today.

Christians have opposed rearmament with concrete action. In the 1960s and 1970s the brothers Daniel and Philip Berrigan, both Catholic priests in the USA, repeatedly made their way into nuclear and missile depots and did damage to the weapons, and they destroyed draft papers during the Vietnam war. They allowed themselves to be arrested and were given long prison sentences by the authorities. They compared the weapons of mass annihilation with the Holocaust and saw it as their duty to act against them with radical non-violent actions: 'We say that Christ requires us to affirm life, to stand up for its integrity and holiness and to resist its misuse and its annihilation.'

Mahatma Gandhi and Vinoba Bhave created an instrument which they used against war and civil war, the Shanti Sena or non-violent peace army. In 1942, when the invasion of India by Japanese troops was imminent and the small British colonial army had already withdrawn, Gandhi proposed a three-stage plan for non-violent action:

1. Before the invasion by the aggressor there was to be a 'counter-invasion' with friendliness, good-will and positive behaviour in the spirit of reconciliation;
2. If this did not lead to success, during the invasion a group of unarmed volunteers was to face the attackers in the hope that this would arouse their conscience;
3. After an invasion absolute non-cooperation with the invaders could undermine their rule.

However, only years later was it possible to put these ideas of Gandhi into practice. Vinoba Bhave founded the Shanti Sena in 1957. Volunteers who met high demands for inner strength and character and had to make an oath of non-violence were trained over many weeks and were active during times of peace in local construction programmes; in times of unrest they were put between members of different religious communities or caste groups, helped refugees in the Bangladeshi war of liberation and supported the reconstruction in the unruly provinces of north-east India.

The concept of the *jihad*, often wrongly translated 'holy war', is strongly disputed among Muslims. Whereas parts of the Muslim world use the term *jihad* to justify the violence of their group, the Thai scholar Chaiwat Satha-Anand points out that in its most general meaning *jihad*, which is derived from a root meaning 'struggle, make an effort', designates an effort or a struggle for righteousness and truth. So the goal of the *jihad* is to end structural violence. Here a distinction is made between the 'lesser *jihad*', struggling with an opponent, and the 'greater *jihad*', struggling with oneself for self-purification. The concept of *jihad* expresses the means of this struggle, thus also of violence and war, on a moral level. The conditions associated with the waging of the 'lesser *jihad*', namely that in its goals and its implementation this is guided by the continuous 'greater *jihad*', makes it impossible to use violence in an age of weapons of mass destruction. From this and from the invitation to Muslims first to use all other means, follows the conclusion that the only legitimate form of the 'lesser *jihad*' which is necessary in cases of injustice or expression is non-violent action. The Iraqi writer Khalid Kishtainy, who lives in London, therefore argues in view of the oppressive situation of most countries with a majority Muslim population: 'If the Islamic world – and the world as a whole – needs anything – then it is a Muslim civil *jihad* which attempts to remove all injustices, corruption and despotism in the Islamic world without having to kill or destroy.'

In a discussion with the Grand Sheikh of Al Azhar University in Cairo, the Malay Muslim human rights activist Ahmad Faiz bin Abdul Rahman opposed any form of terrorism. Granted, Mohammed Sayyed Tantawi stated that suicide attacks which injure or kill non-combatants are incompatible with Islamic war.

But in the same sentence he qualified this again by saying that one must ask Palestinian assassins what has motivated them. For there are such events in a war of liberation. The discussion makes it clear that the return to non-violent means of carrying on the struggle for justice is the preferred option in Islam. Clayton Ramey, a US Muslim, criticizes the arms trade and rearmament and thinks that they are incompatible with Islamic commandments. According to Ramey, it is this question which decides whether a human being can actualize and maintain the relationship to God, as God's trustee and despite his weaknesses.

Buddhism shows that the discussion about readiness for war has not spared any religious community. On closer inspection, the notion of many people in the West that Buddhist societies are shaped by ideas of non-violence must be revised, although the principle of non-violence is deeply rooted in Buddhism. In his autobiography, the Dalai Lama describes Tibetan society before the occupation by Chinese troops as shaken by unrest and rebellions. Buddhists concerned for peace feel that the attitude of the Buddhist monastic order in Sri Lanka to the civil war which has lasted since 1983 is highly problematical, as time and again monks have forced Sri Lankan politicians to adopt a harsh attitude towards the Tamil Republic on the island and not to give way in negotiations with the rebels. Only a small minority among them raise their voices for a balance which would call for concessions from the Buddhist Singhalese to the Tamils. Instead of this, the bloodshed has continued, supported by the chauvinism of the monks, who fear that they and the Singhalese will lose influence. Only a few monks went on a peace march in spring 1995 into the state of Jaffna, then held by rebels, to indicate their concern for peace and their readiness for dialogue.

Women and men

When women in South Africa came to an important prayer meeting in the mosque on the twenty-seventh day of Ramadan, the month of fasting, in 1994, men had already occupied the women's prayer room on the first floor. A tent had been built for the women. But the women were not happy about this, and under the leadership of Shamima Shaikh occupied their room. Shaikh did not stop at this achievement, but demanded that women should not have to pray in separate rooms. Along with other women and men she founded her own prayer meeting, in which equality of the sexes was striven for. The battle waged for equal rights for Muslim women by Shamima Shaikh, who died prematurely at the beginning of 1998, did not end with her death. At her wish a friend said the prayers for the dead in her home – in the history of the Muslim world there are only a few examples of such public appearances by women. Women were also represented at the subsequent prayers in the mosque and at the cemetery – in Muslim societies the funeral is almost always restricted to men.

It is probably no coincidence that women like Shamima Shaikh appear in particular in South Africa, where the battle against apartheid has sensitized people to questions of justice. Her concern is shared and supported by a South African Muslim who has argued for the equal rights of men and women, Farid Esack (see above, pp. 60–4). He thinks it necessary for Muslim men in particular to abandon their apologetic attitude and look the oppression of women in the Muslim tradition in the face. In his estimation, discrimination against women and their dehumanization says a great deal about how serious Muslims are about becoming 'Allah's witnesses' in questions of justice: 'Muslim men use the argument that Islam gave women rights fourteen hundred years ago to deny them the exercising of these rights in our societies.' The mere notion of having to 'give' women rights points in the wrong direction. For him the decisive question is how traditional and religious texts, above all the Qur'an, can be read to overcome patriarchal patterns, for it is not only the wrong practice of Muslims which discriminates against women but also Muslim law, which has not developed adequately. Esack puts in question the current interpretation of the principle of the impossibility of changing tradition and the text of the Qur'an: 'Both were active within a given society and were also the product of that society, a society which Allah wanted to see changed. It is this transformation and this vision of freedom and justice, rooted in Allah's will for all men and women, for which we strive – instead of obsessively clinging to a familiar life-style which today is presented as immutable.'

In her books *The Political Harem* and *The Sultana*, Fatima Mernissi (see above, pp. 69–72) attempted to assimilate the past and reappropriate religious tradition. She investigated the historical contexts of statements about the relationship between women and men in terms of its relationship to Muslim sources and wrote: 'I have found a feminist prophet and brought her to mind from the darkness of the past.' This is not an apologetics which seeks to veil traditions which are hostile to women. As a woman, Mernissi wants to make a contribution to the discussion of the involvement of women in social life on the basis of equal rights. According to Mernissi, resistance to this and to the recognition of the rich heritage of women in the tradition and in the present derives from men who reject critical, rational thought and call for submission and obedience. The Muslim women's movement is therefore also very important for the just shaping of Muslim societies generally, for the suppression of free expression of opinion and independent thinking is directed against all, women and men.

According to Mernissi, orthodoxy is particularly opposed to the critical voices of women because these are offering most prominent resistance against the ruling order. The Pakistani scholar Suroosh Irfani notes with disapproval that so few Muslim men are critical of the violation of human rights by the Taliban regime in

Afghanistan. Along with the Pakistani national poet Muhammad Iqbal, she therefore calls with great urgency for a new investigation of the concepts of 'uncritical observance of rules', 'traditional practice' and 'literal interpretation of religious sources'. 'Without the restoration of subjectivity which this demand entails, a large part of Muslim will remain a hostage of its own internal Taliban.'

Fatima Ahmed Ibrahim from Sudan, founder of the Sudanese Women's Union and in 1964 the first woman in the Sudanese parliament, points out that it is high time for women to become aware of their rights, for them to take part in the interpretation of women's texts, for 'Women do not make any decisions. Who is responsible for this situation? Neither Islam nor Christianity, but the political regimes which are in power.' Fatima Ibrahim therefore always sees the link between discrimination against women and the general situation of human rights.

Many Muslim women and women supporters of human rights do not have a religious motivation but a secular motivation: they include the Pakistani lawyer Asma Jahangir, the Egyptian writer Nawal el-Saadawi, the Kurd Laila Zana and the Bengali author Taslima Nasrim. Nasrim, who openly professes a non-religious humanism, was exposed to persecution because of her attack on religious intolerance on the south Asian sub-continent and had to leave her homeland of Bangladesh. As a founder member of the Women's Action Forum and the President of the Pakistani Human Rights Organization, Jahangir is attacking the discrimination against women and minorities. As she also defends people who are also accused under the blasphemy law, which even carries the death penalty, Asma Jahangir receives murder threats. Islam is used as a weapon against women like her to prevent her from making unpopular statements.

'The most important questions of a rising feminist theology to the ruling theology are iconoclastic. They attack phallocratic fantasies, the worship of power. Why do men worship a God whose most important quality is power, whose interest is subjection and whose fear is equal rights? . . . Why should we worship and love a being who does not transcend the moral level of the culture determined by people of a particular time but stabilizes it?' This question from the Christian theologian Dorothee Sölle (see pp. 45–9) also speaks to the situation of Muslim women described above. In her thoughts on a feminist theology, a liberation theology which challenges the real political, economic, intellectual, physical and psychological violations and mutilations of women, she raises and discusses the question: 'Does God also take place among us? In the process of becoming aware, on the way from the nothingness which society imposes on us, the question whether we need God is dug up from the rubble of tradition. I often have the impression that the longing for transcendence which there is speaks most clearly in the fears and desperation of women.'

In connection with the churches' Conciliar Process for Justice, Peace and the Preservation of Creation, in 1990 the Protestant theologian Elisabeth Raiser remarked that the traditional patriarchal world order is the origin of the present crisis. Raiser was a member of the executive committee of the European Ecumenical Assembly in Basel in 1989. According to Raiser, sexism underlies other problems like injustice, militarism and war; the destruction of the environment; and the attack on women's capacity for reproduction. Therefore the women who are involved in the conciliar process want the phenomenon of sexism also to be put on the churches' agenda.

(Since then, dialogue between Christian women of the so-called First World and the so-called Third World within the framework of the ecumenical movement has made it clear that white Western feminists – including those in the churches – have not always escaped the prevailing traditions of thought in their own society and for example are continuing its racism or its claims to social or economic predominance. So a broad movement of 'Third World' women theologians has come into being who have made their own situation the starting point for their analyses and actions in order to work for the renewal of their churches. Some important names are Elsa Tamez of Costa Rica, Julia Esquival of Guatemala, Aruna Gnanadason of India, Virginia Fabella of the Philippines, Marie Therese Porcile of Uruguay and Chung Hyun Kyung of South Korea.)

Women from Hindu cultural circles see themselves faced with similar tasks. They have struggled critically with the relationship of Mahatma Gandhi to his wife Kasturba and also investigated the role of women in the Indian independence movement. The bulk of the feminist movement in India has a secular motivation and does not refer much to Hindu symbols; it even quite deliberately dissociates itself from Hindu practices like the burning of women and the exclusion of urban middle-class women from public life. For the movement, the revival of these practices is an expression of the social crisis of India which has also led to the success of Hindu fundamentalist parties. Some women's groups have adopted powerful symbols, like the powerful – and sometimes violent – goddess Kali. She represents female energy and power (Sanskrit *shakti*). The role of the main female figure of the heroic epic Ramayana – her name is Sita – has been investigated by the feminist Bina Agarwal: in her poem 'Sita, speak,' she calls on Sita and thus women to go public and to depict their part of reality.

In Sri Lanka, Burma, Laos, Cambodia and Thailand, the lands of Theravada Buddhism, there have not been ordained nuns for several centuries. A new foundation of orders of nuns comes up against legal regulations of the order which have also prevented Mahayana nuns being recognized in these countries. In Sri Lanka the 'Upasikas', ordained laywomen who like Buddhist monks have bald heads and wear robes, are treated with much less respect than their brothers in the faith. Although they do important social work particularly in the economically backward regions of the deep south of the tropical island, whereas a large proportion of the monks perform predominantly ritual tasks in the village temples, they are largely denied public recognition.

The Thai Buddhist Chatsuman Kabilsingh describes how in a situation in which the modernization of the societies of South-East Asia and their globalization is having an incomparably greater impact on women, the new foundation of an order of nuns could not only result in a strengthening of Buddhism in the land but have an important social function. She attacks the traditional idea that women in Buddhism cannot attain spiritual liberation in the same way as men. The editor of the Discourses of Buddha maintained these and other patriarchal notions of Indian antiquity. According to Kabilsingh, as also in Christianity and Islam, here too a critical reading of the texts in context is necessary, in order to separate the teaching from the conditions in which it arose, conditions which run counter to the liberating attitude of the religion itself. As these restrictions on the status of women are still interwoven into the distribution of power in Buddhist societies, Buddhist organizations too must subject themselves to critical investigation. The impossibility of ordaining nuns is also connected in particular with the tradition of having sons ordained in order to acquire religious merit while at the same time sending daughters into the city for prostitution or dependent work to support the usually poor families.

The organization Sakyadhita, i.e. Buddha's Daughters, which was founded in 1987, brings together ordained and non-ordained women from different Buddhist countries in order to work towards creating a community of nuns in the lands of Theravada Buddhism. The involvement of women in the interpretation and administration of the Buddhist heritage, the possibility of entrusting problems which have arisen in the course of the modernization of their country – prostitution and other forms of sexual exploitation, social oppression, disadvantages in education – to Buddhist women religious orders would also give new relevance to Buddhism in these countries. Particularly because this would favour independent models of development, it would be an advantage for the whole of society.

INDEX OF NAMES

Figures in **bold** indicate the main discussion of the person concerned.

SUBJECT INDEX